National Interest

Key Concepts in Political Science

GENERAL EDITOR: Leonard B. Schapiro

EXECUTIVE EDITOR: Peter Calvert

Other titles in the same series include:

ALREADY PUBLISHED

Martin Albrow	**Bureaucracy**
Peter Calvert	**Revolution**
Ioan Davies	**Social Mobility and Political Change**

IN PREPARATION

Shlomo Avinieri	**Utopianism**
Stanley Benn	**Power**
Anthony H. Birch	**Representation**
Brian Chapman	**Police State**
Karl Deutsch	**Legitimacy**
S. E. Finer	**Dictatorship**
C. J. Friedrich	**Tradition and Authority**
Julius Gould	**Violence**
E. Kamenka and Alice Erh-Soon Tay	**Law**
J. F. Lively	**Democracy**
Robert Orr	**Liberty**
P. H. Partridge	**Consent and Consensus**
John Plamenatz	**Ideology**
John C. Rees	**Equality**
Bernard Schaffer	**Modernization**
Leonard B. Schapiro	**Totalitarianism**
Henry Tudor	**Political Myth**

National Interest

Joseph Frankel
University of Southampton

Praeger Publishers

New York · Washington · London

Praeger Publishers, Inc.
111 Fourth Avenue, New York, N.Y. 10003, U.S.A.
5 Cromwell Place, London sw7, England
Published in the United States of America in 1970
by Praeger Publishers, Inc.

Library of Congress Catalog Card Number: 75-100913

Printed in Great Britain

Contents

'Key Concepts'
an Introductory Note

Political concepts are part of our daily speech—we abuse 'bureaucracy' and praise 'democracy', welcome or recoil from 'revolution'. Emotive words such as 'equality', 'dictatorship', 'élite' or even 'power' can often, by the very passions which they raise, obscure a proper understanding of the sense in which they are, or should be, or should not be, or have been used. Confucius regarded the 'rectification of names' as the first task of government. 'If names are not correct, language will not be in accordance with the truth of things', and this in time would lead to the end of justice, to anarchy and to war. One could with some truth point out that the attempts hitherto by governments to enforce their own quaint meanings on words have not been conspicuous for their success in the advancement of justice. 'Rectification of names' there must certainly be: but most of us would prefer such rectification to take place in the free debate of the university, in the competitive arena of the pages of the book or journal.

Analysis of commonly used political terms, their reassessment or their 'rectification', is, of course, normal activity in the political science departments of our universities. The idea of this series was indeed born in the course of discussion between a few university teachers of political science, of whom Professor S. E. Finer of Manchester University was one. It occurred to us that a series of short books, discussing the 'Key Concepts' in political science would serve two purposes. In universities these books could provide the kind of brief political texts which might be of assistance to students in gaining a fuller understanding of the terms which they were constantly using. But we also hoped that outside the universities there exists a reading public which has the time, the curiosity and the inclination to pause to reflect on some of those words and ideas which are so often taken for granted. Perhaps even 'that insidious and crafty animal', as Adam Smith described

the politician and statesman, will occasionally derive some plea-
sure or even profit from that more leisurely analysis which academic study can afford, and which a busy life in the practice of
politics often denies.

It has been very far from the minds of those who have been
concerned in planning and bringing into being the 'Key
Concepts' series to try and impose (as if that were possible!) any
uniform pattern on the authors who have contributed, or will
contribute, to it. I, for one, hope that each author will, in his
own individual manner, seek and find the best way of helping us
to a fuller understanding of the concept which he has chosen to
analyse. But whatever form the individual exposition may take,
there are, I believe, three aspects of illumination which we can
confidently expect from each volume in this series. First, we can
look for some examination of the history of the concept, and of its
evolution against a changing social and political background. I
believe, as many do who are concerned with the study of political
science, that it is primarily in history that the explanation must
be sought for many of the perplexing problems of political analysis and judgement which beset us today. Second, there is the
semantic aspect. To look in depth at a 'key concept' necessarily
entails a study of the name which attached itself to it; of the different ways in which, and the different purposes for which, the
name was used; of the way in which in the course of history the
same name was applied to several concepts, or several names
were applied to one and the same concept; and, indeed, of the
changes which the same concept, or what appears to be the same
concept, has undergone in the course of time. This analysis will
usually require a searching examination of the relevant literature
in order to assess the present stage of scholarship in each particular field. And thirdly, I hope that the reader of each volume in
this series will be able to decide for himself what the proper and
valid use should be of a familiar term in politics, and will gain, as
it were, from each volume a sharper and better-tempered tool of
political analysis.

There are many today who would disagree with Bismarck's
view that politics can never be an exact science. I express no
opinion on this much debated question. But all of us who are

students of politics—and our numbers both inside and outside the universities continue to grow—will be the better for knowing what precisely we mean when we use a common political term.

London School of Economics   Leonard B. Schapiro
and Political Science   General Editor

Preface

This volume is written in the Aristotelian tradition of political theory, with a strong behavioural bias. The argument is structured around a logical analysis of the major aspects of the concept of 'national interest' but, to avoid being abstruse, it is profusely illustrated with examples drawn from contemporary state practice. Whenever possible suggestions are made for further empirical research because, in contrast to most other key political concepts, that of 'national interest' has been so far only little explored.

I would like to thank Mr. Timothy Hawkins for assisting me with the survey of the relevant literature; the Social Science Research Council for financing an extensive research visit to Asia in 1969 which enabled me to develop comparatively several of this book's themes; and, most of all, my wife for her patience in helping me to reduce, as far as possible, the abstruseness of the argument.

The Old Rectory,
Avington, Hants.   September 1969

Part I
The Meaning of the Concept

1/Meanings, History and Usages

Meanings

'National interest' is a singularly vague concept. It assumes a variety of meanings in the various contexts in which it is used and, despite its fundamental importance, these meanings often cannot be reconciled; hence no agreement can be reached about its ultimate meaning. The admittedly limited literature specifically dealing with it[1] suggests no clear-cut classification of its various uses. It is characteristic that no entry under the heading can be found in the Oxford Dictionaries, in the first edition of *The International Encyclopaedia of Social Sciences* (1935) or in *A Dictionary of Social Sciences* (1965).

Fundamental but relatively unimportant is the semantic ambiguity stemming from the fact that the adjective 'national' refers both to the nation which is a social group and to the state which denotes its political organization. In most cases reference is made to the state and it is usually clear from the context when this is not the case, e.g. when the argument is about nationalism, or a nation devoid of a state, or when the nation is juxtaposed to the state, etc. Ambiguities can, however, occur and can be of great importance, e.g. when a nation is not coterminous with its national state, as in the case of the interwar Germans or of the contemporary Chinese.

Professor Rosenau has proposed a distinction between the use of the concept for the purpose of political analysis and that of political action.

As an analytic tool, it is employed to describe, explain, or evaluate the sources or the adequacy of a nation's foreign policy. As an instrument of political action, it serves as a means of justifying, denouncing or proposing policies. Both usages, in other words, refer to what is best for a national society. They also share a tendency to confine the intended meaning to what is best for a national society. Beyond these general considerations, however, the two uses of the concept have little in common.[2]

This analytical distinction appeals to common sense, but does not offer the means for further logical analysis or for empirical investigation. First, when an individual speaks of 'national interest' it is often impossible to decide in which of these two senses he is using the concept. One can be guided by his role or position but this simple criterion is insufficient. Those directly involved in political action, such as statesmen, politicians or senior civil servants, do not restrict themselves to action but habitually engage in analysis; neither are the professional academics and the publicists necessarily divorced from political action. There was no clear dividing line between the arguments of President Johnson and Walter Lippmann or of Robert MacNamara and Hermann Kahn; Henry Kissinger both analysed and was politically active, whether as an independent academic critic of President Johnson's Vietnam policy or as the White House adviser of President Nixon.

Second, within each argument, by whomever it is made, there is no clear-cut distinction between these two uses of the concept. For instance, when we discuss whether it is in the national interest of a member of the North Atlantic Treaty Organization, to maintain the organization, this involves both the *discussion* of NATO as an instrument of national strategy and a *prescription*, be it to maintain or to reduce defences against Soviet communism. Both are found in all analyses although in greatly varying proportions and occasionally only in an implied form.

Two fundamentally different approaches to the analyses of the concept are represented by the 'objectivists' and the 'subjectivists'. The former assume that national interest can be objectively defined, or, at least, can be examined with the help of some objectively definable yardsticks and criteria. The latter interpret it as a constantly changing pluralistic set of subjective preferences; the most important recent work in this direction has been through the study of decision making. It is impossible to reconcile the two approaches and frequently even the individual contributions within one of the schools.

A parallel distinction can be made between the approaches of the behaviourists and of the ecologists. Neither commends itself in its extreme form. Thus in the most articulate dialogue about national interest, the political debates between the 'realists' and the 'idealists' in the United States, the participants were characteristically reluctant '. . . to conceive of the national interest as being whatever the most powerful nationals say it is and by the ease with which the flag of "the national interest" can be hoisted over what seems to be, in the final analysis, only personal preference.'[3]

The definition of national interest further depends upon the position a person takes up between several pairs of extremes, such as altruistic-egoistic (ideals *v.* self-interest, idealists *v.* realists), short- and long-term concerns, activist-reactive, radical-conservative, hard- and tender-minded, traditional-innovating, collectivist-individualist, etc. etc. In all cases it is more profitable to think not of a dichotomy but of a spectrum within which the attitudes of individuals can be ranked after they have been measured by some empirical indices.

Finally, the increasingly blurred boundary between the domestic and the international activities of the state adds to the confusion since values pursued within these two areas of activity are not necessarily identical and often receive quite different priorities.

The confusion is so great and the policy objectives remain so frequently hidden behind the verbal flannel of political argument that some political scientists are tempted to dismiss the concept altogether. Raymond Aron, for instance, gives up the attempt at its rational definition, regarding it as either a formula vague to the point of being meaningless or a pseudo-theory.[4] James S. Rosenau in the quoted entry in *Encyclopaedia of Social Sciences* shares this scepticism. On the other hand, the majority of political scientists attach considerable political significance to the concept; especially articulate are Hans Morgenthau and Arnold Wolfers.

The decision-making analysis offers a relatively uncontroversial approach to the meaning of the concept. Whether considered an independent, a mediating or a dependent variable, or just a rationalization, 'national interest' constitutes an element in the making of foreign policy to which, however it may be defined, statesmen profess to attach great importance. In the last century Palmerston confidently pronounced, 'We have no eternal allies, and we have no eternal enemies. Our interests are eternal, and those interests it is our duty to follow.' In our own generation this was matched by President de Gaulle's pronouncing that nations have no feelings but only interests.

If foreign policy is defined as 'a formulation of desired outcomes which are intended (or expected) to be consequent upon decisions adopted (or made) by those who have authority (or ability) to commit the machinery of the state and a significant fraction of national resources to that end',[5] national interest describes the desired outcomes. It has been tersely and acceptably defined by the Brookings Institution as 'the general and continuing ends for which a nation acts'.[6]

The substantive definition in each case must be arrived at through confronting the aspirations of the state with its image of the international environment and all the ensuing uncertainties can be subsumed under three major headings:

1 Vagueness of the aspirations and lack of clear priorities;

2 Incomplete knowledge of the international environment;

3 Uncertainties about the behaviour of other states and the evolution of the international system.

The third difficulty can be eliminated only by improving the structure of international relations as the efforts of individual states to insulate themselves through accumulating power are becoming increasingly less successful. Analysis of national interests can be legitimately confined to the first two headings to which it can contribute at least as a partial clarification.

Such analysis in general terms assumes that, in some essential respects, generalizations are warranted. One may, indeed postulate that, 'the national interests of all states are broadly similar. They are centred upon the welfare of the nation and the preservation of its political doctrine and national style of life.'[7] This assumption is not invalidated by the fact that the stakes pursued by individual states are extremely diverse and not at all permanent—compare the search for space by the Nazis and the Japanese in the interwar period or the western anti-Communist policies after the last war. This diversity and impermanence sufficiently impressed Raymond Aron to make him deny the existence of a rational national interest altogether.[8] Within each separate context the interests of each single state are bound to be individual and, moreover, we cannot expect, even within the state, general agreement about their contents.

National interests are often expected to be permanent or extremely durable. In our generation, Hans Morgenthau has matched Lord Palmerston's assertions on the subject: 'The national interest of great powers and in good measure the methods by which it is to be secured are impervious to ideological and institutional changes.'[9] Their permanence is, however, only relative. They are subject to reinterpretation, especially in the light of changes in power relations. Since the last war, for example, Britain has abandoned her traditional oceanic priorities and the principle of avoiding military commitment to the Continent in peace time; the meaning of the

Monroe Doctrine, reinterpreted several times since its announcement in 1826, has again changed; the western anti-Communist
and apparently also the Soviet anti-capitalist interests have been
greatly attenuated.

History and usages

The history[10] of the concept of 'national interest' goes
back to the earliest stages of the evolution of the modern state,
in the sixteenth and seventeenth centuries, first in Italy and then
in England. After the advent of nationalism, the older terms—the
'will of the prince', 'dynastic interests' or *raison d'état*—were
gradually replaced by reference to the nation. The term 'national
interest' has been extensively used by American statesmen ever
since the establishment of the Constitution. Similar terms were
concurrently employed, such as 'national honour', 'public
interest', 'general will'; often the imperative nature of the concept was stressed by reference to 'vital interests'.

It is scarcely possible to trace the early history of 'national
interest' much further back. Primitive societies, when engaged
in sporadic contacts, must have already developed some notions
of self-interest based upon survival, securing power and wealth,
but it is likely that they conceived it within specific bargaining
or conflict situations rather than in general terms. In ancient
Greece, the concept could not be articulated because of the
absence of clear-cut political boundaries and of the modern distinctions between political and cultural communities. The
Greeks generally conceived their interests within the orbit of
their individual city-states, much as did the Renaissance Italians.
During the Persian Wars these were, however, subordinated to
pan-Hellenic ideas; in the thinking of the Stoics, both were
blurred by the broader concept of a Hellenic cultural community, universal in the sense of embracing all the civilized
world. This blurring of differences between national and universal took a political shape in the near-universal Roman
Empire. In the Middle Ages the confused relations between the

Trans- national
interests - but
equal convergence of interests

individual political units and the Holy Roman Empire as well as the confusion between politics and metaphysics offered no scope for the evolution of the idea of 'national interest'.

In the West today the 'nation' and 'national interest' are losing their supreme place in politics. On the one hand a unitary national interest strikes us as inappropriate for our pluralist societies; on the other, it clashes with global ideals. The clarity of the concept of 'national interest' is closely connected with that of political boundaries and hence the generally perceived crisis of the national state inevitably leads to a crisis of national interest. Its popular appeal is waning. In the 1960s the concept became distinctly unpopular in the Europe of the Six as an archaic obstacle to integration; in the United States owing to its abuse in the futile Vietnamese involvement; in the United Kingdom because of its frequent invocation by Prime Minister Harold Wilson as a means for rallying the people to accept hardships and for castigating those who opposed unsuccessful governmental policies.

Simultaneously, however, national interest has grown in importance in the foreign policies of Communist states. It provides an increasingly more convincing alternative model to an ideological explanation of Soviet foreign policy which, in defiance of ideological alignment, is rapidly increasing its hostility to China and is groping towards a 'security community' with the United States. It is clearly the basis of the pressures in Eastern Europe to abandon rigid reliance upon the Soviet pattern and to embark upon national roads to socialism and on more independent foreign policies.

Even clearer is the crucial importance of national interest as a basis for the formulation of the foreign policies of new states, especially those in really difficult situations. For instance, President Banda of Malawi in his address to Parliament on October 8, 1968, announced that the only criterion he applied to his relations with other states was the fact of existence or non-existence of areas of common interest from which mutual benefits might be derived. These relations should not be governed by the colour or race of those controlling other states or by their domestic policies.[11] Particularly interesting is the case of Singapore, a city-state which did not aspire to independence but was forced to accept it in 1965 when it was asked to leave the Federation of Malaysia. Its prime minister, Mr. Lee Kuan-Yew, and his foreign minister Mr. S. Rajaratman, are exceptionally articulate and have been engaged in a continuous search for the definition of Singapore's national interests.

All writers on foreign policy employ the concept, directly or indirectly; signal early examples are Machiavelli and Bolingbroke. As a widespread scholarly pursuit, foreign policy analysis did not, however, fully develop until this century, and in particular not until after 1945.[12] Looking in retrospect at the 1930s, we find that many thinkers, especially historians, employed, explicitly or implicitly, the yardstick of 'national interest' to measure and evaluate the policies of the various countries, especially the 'Appeasement Policy' in Britain and the involvement by the United States in the Second World War. They postulated that such interest is a matter of objective reality. Some political scientists, such as Hans Morgenthau, denied this but used the concept to analyse foreign policy behaviour; particularly important among them were those who adopted the decision-making approach introduced by L. C. Snyder.

Any statement or analysis concerned with the purpose of foreign policy or with the values pursued by it inevitably refers to national interest. Nevertheless, the vagueness of the concept, the complete lack of agreement about its definition and the absence of empirical indicators, have precluded its rigorous use. It is possible to argue, as Professor Rosenau does, that we cannot usefully employ it analytically and must merely take cognizance of its employment in political action, use it as a datum requiring analysis. Even so, the boundary between the use of an 'analytic concept' and the investigation of a 'datum' is not fully clear-cut. Perhaps we can best understand a baffling datum by trying to isolate it and to use it as an organizing concept even if the task is overwhelmingly difficult and the chances of full success are ever so slight.

The concept of 'national interest' is particularly useful for purposes of comparison. Such comparison used to be simple in the nineteenth century when the Concert of Europe consisted of a few, fairly homogeneous states. It has now become increasingly complex owing to the combination of several developments. First, the multiplication of states limits the uses of detailed historical inquiry since *all* the 140 or more states are obviously beyond anybody's scope. Second, a parallel multiplication of cultures and of value-systems obstructs understanding. Instead of being, as in the past, a major tool of analysis in the circumscribed western world, historical analogy has become less useful and even misleading when we try to understand the foreign policies of a Communist, or Asian or African state. Third, the constantly growing volume and scope of international transactions has broadened the field of enquiry. Fourth, the integration of international politics has greatly reduced the value of limited comparisons.

The problems of comparison are serious even between relatively similar states in one region, such as Scandinavia or Central America. They are overwhelming in broader spheres as shown when one tries to compare entries in world-wide collections of foreign policy analyses.[13] Nevertheless, despite all their dissimilarities, owing to the increased integration of the international system within which they are operating, the states are bound also to develop further *similarities*.

Taxonomies and comparisons of foreign policy can centre upon such important characteristics as capabilities,[14] political regimes, ideologies, degrees of economic development, diplomatic styles, etc.[15] In the subsequent argument special attention will be paid to two customary classifications: into 'superpowers', 'middle powers', and 'small states', and into Western-liberal, Communist, and new states (or the Third World). Only one

traditional taxonomy centres upon the purposes of foreign policy
—that distinguishing between the *status quo* and the revisionist
states. This useful classification is still awaiting further development and refinement which is most likely to be achieved within
the context of the analysis of international systems.

Purpose of foreign policy

It has never been easy to establish the purpose of foreign
policy. Nevertheless, ignoring its purpose is just as unhelpful as
a limited behaviourist analysis of the behaviour of the individual.
When we exclude all voluntarist and teleological elements we
can clarify the mechanical elements of behaviour but we clearly
fail to explain human behaviour as a whole. Likewise, a purely
behavioural appraisal of foreign policy is inadequate as it cannot be used for moral and political evaluations which are considered important in all political systems. It does not really
matter whether we postulate unconscious purpose based
upon impulse[16] or conscious purpose based upon rational
processes.

The general confusion in the analysis of foreign policy between aspirations and actual policies[17] is detrimental to the
clear grasp of the notion of 'purpose'. Caution is clearly indicated in assuming that every single policy serves some national
interest as these interests frequently remain vague and obscure.
There is a deep gap between such vague general values as
sovereignty, independence or freedom and any concrete policy
objective. 'National interest', as employed in political argument, is frequently far-fetched although rarely, if ever, meaningless. The fashionable 'systems analysis' which explains the purpose of foreign policy in terms of a general striving of all systems
to reduce disequilibria to the minimum, at least provides a starting point. Seen from this angle, all foreign policy is goal-seeking,
even if the decision makers are only dimly aware or even completely unaware of this. Its basic objective is to reduce all
domestic disequilibria.

In general terms, assuming purpose in a social organization as distinct from the persons acting on its behalf, attributes to this organization certain anthropomorphic features which are inevitably misleading. In the post-war years, adherents of the structural-functional and systems analysis schools have been analysing states in abstract organizational terms and have been attributing to them, as systems, such propensities as 'boundary' or 'system-maintenance'. The notion of 'purpose' really refers to the individual decision makers; it is meaningful for the state considered as a system only in so far as the decision makers share a common purpose or set of purposes. In all cases this extends to the continuation or self-preservation of the system. Beyond that the position varies according to the behaviour of the decision makers: the state may appear to have a sense of direction, or not; it may appear to have a goal at one time but not at another; it may suddenly change goal priorities, etc.[18]

To turn to specific groups of states, the behaviour of *new states*, deviating as it does from the traditional patterns of foreign policy, both western and Communist, is to us frequently perplexing. The various explanations of its purpose in terms of striving for independence, participation, economic growth, equality, or a combination of these, are all unconvincingly broad rationalizations which, moreover, are couched in a terminology transferred from another political culture and not fully appropriate to the states involved.

The purpose of *Communist* foreign policy used to be fairly straightforward: the Soviet Union was striving at the communization of the world which, on the whole, coincided with her power-political objectives. With the disintegration of the Communist bloc the purpose has become confused. Is, for instance, the Soviet Union still trying to communize the Third World or is she more concerned with denying it to the Chinese? Similarly, in *the West*, the six members of the European communities are uncertainly hovering on the brink of closer integration whereas 'the Anglo-Saxon countries' have now lost their 'moral opportunity';[19] neither the United States nor the United Kingdom feel that they are in a position to pursue broad moral purposes, rather than narrow self-interest. Neither country has managed to define this self-interest and hence it is difficult to regard much of their foreign policies as exactly purposeful.

Thus it appears that foreign policy is generally pursued without any clear purpose. Most policies are reactive, following real or imagined stimuli from the environment; active foreign policy which positively pursues objectives based upon firmly held values, is much rarer. Underlying all these changes is the growing limitation of state-power. Despite its physical escalation, this power has become increasingly less adequate to secure the objectives of foreign policy; the United States failure in Vietnam is the most striking example.

The question must be raised whether freedom and purpose may not be most easily found when a country is relatively powerless. De Gaulle's France may be looked at in this light and the study of the policies of small states,[20] particularly of those pursued by the diplomatic leaders of the Third World, is here relevant. An analysis of purpose can therefore directly contribute to the understanding of power, especially of the relationship between military and diplomatic power.

Problems of methodology

'National interest' is the most comprehensive description of the whole value complex of foreign policy. It is also an exceptionally unclear concept. Like all other difficult concepts it gives rise to the temptation to go to extremes. We can say that it is intractable, beyond our power of analysis, and hence rely on our intuition; if determined to be 'scientific', we can simplify and modify the concept, break it up into elements and components until it becomes manageable, hoping that the analysed concept is still identical with the real one. An attempt is made here to pursue the second approach while avoiding its extremes. This can be done first, by trying to be explicit about the relationship between the proposed simplified categories and real life through an extensive use of concrete examples and, second, by seeking the most promising ways for establishing empirical indicators for the propositions advanced. Although satisfactory knowledge based upon a rigorous scientific method and clear definitions seems unattainable, we can at least seek a subjective guide to the investigation of the purposes of foreign policy. Our argument may not pass the stringent criteria applicable to a theory but should help us to organize the field and leave out or fail to explain as few elements as possible; even if not fully acceptable to others, it may still help us to find a basis for rational discussion.

The most promising solution seems to lie in employing clearly defined models[21] which concentrate upon one or a few dimensions selected as independent variables, leaving other significant and frequently still unexplored dimensions as constants. As long as such models are constructed with the full awareness of their artificiality, they need not blind us to national interest as a whole. The dangers of concentrating upon one model are, however, great. Thus, for instance, in the perennial debates on 'guns or butter' which recur in all political systems, models of the national interest defined either in predominantly economic or in predominantly strategic terms are widely employed. Even if scientifically quite rigorous, these alternate models are politically unconvincing. They cannot be reconciled except on the basis of a broader conception of the national interest, incorporating both; unfortunately the theories of international relations supply no clues for our search of the meaning of national interest as a whole.

The purpose of this book is neither to prove nor to disprove that there is or should be purpose in foreign policy which can be called 'national interest' but merely to clarify the concept and to demonstrate that it is possible to organize around it our thinking about the purpose of foreign policy and about international behaviour in general. Although the slant is behavioural and not philosophical or normative, the method is only marginally so. As with most international phenomena, it is extremely difficult to identify a 'population' of behavioural events, to draw useful samples and to classify and scale them. This is rather an exercise in pre-empirical but scientific thinking which aims at producing hypotheses and models to be then checked against evidence.

In this initial stage the approach is largely a matter of trained intuition. The application of the concept of the 'national interest' to the actual conduct of foreign policy needs to be explored before we attempt a full explanation of the concept. The first step lies in a systematic description and arrangement of the empirical data available, as compatible as possible with other approaches to the study of foreign policy so as to enable us to profit by their insights. This should lay the foundations for the identification of variables which are both valid and reliable; the key construct should be as operational and as quantifiable as possible.[22] It would, however, be foolhardy to hope for extensive quantification as only some, mainly economic factors are quantifiable, and they must be compared with other, non-quantifiable factors. For example, it is impossible to set off, except in fairly general terms, the economic advantages to be gained from trading with a hostile state against the disadvantages of strengthening it or to decide how highly we should rate the ensuing reduction in hostility. The occasional exercises in quantification lead to inconclusive results. Thus in annual budget debates we translate broad national security policies into specific programmes which are vetted on the basis of their anticipated costs; cost-effectiveness analysis is applied to military expenditure. It is difficult to envisage that these unsatisfactory techniques which enable western political systems to deal with major aspects of defence will be usefully applied more widely.

The analysis of national interest should help to clarify the purpose, dynamism and direction of foreign policy in several ways:

1 By defining the vision of the good life and providing the yardsticks for the evaluation of aspirations;

2 By comparing aspirations with actual policies;

3 By offering the only generally employed criterion for the evaluation of foreign policy;

4 By anticipating explanations and rationalization which are usually couched in terms of national interest.

Since the majority of other approaches centres upon capabilities and constraints, we may hope for some new insights.

The first specific objective of the study is to assist in the analysis of the foreign policy of any single state: to understand the purposive elements of this policy (and incidentally to open an opportunity for pursuing them more successfully); to compare the evolution of the notion of 'national interest' across different periods of time; and to compare the treatment of single issues of foreign policy. Second, in the analysis of inter-state relations, the specific objective is to use national interest as an organizing concept for the comparison of foreign policies; to compare factor by factor the foreign policies of pairs of inter-acting states, whether friendly, or hostile, or neutral; and to compare the treatment by several states of similar or identical issues of foreign policy.

The major aim of this inquiry is taxonomic, to break down the concept of national interest into factors which may be ultimately used in factor-analysis, but some questions are asked and some tentative hypotheses are formulated in the process. In fact, there is no intrinsic difference between description, correlation and explanation. On the contrary, they represent a continuum in which correlations are no more than descriptions of two or three co-varying factors, while explanations are no more than detailed descriptions in which correlations are closely interconnected to the point of being compelling to those who are scientifically concerned with the phenomena investigated.[23] Obviously description must precede explanation and therefore further progress requires the application of this scheme to the study of as many individual states as possible.

2/Analytical Distinctions and Theories

The major distinctions proposed

The method by which we classify social phenomena is indicated less by their nature than by the aims of our analysis. No existing taxonomy, including that proposed by Professor Rosenau, is convenient for the comparative study of foreign policy which is the major objective of this book. Hence I would like to propose a new classification of the uses of the term 'national interest' into *aspirational, operational* and *explanatory and polemical*. The logic of this classification is highly imperfect since the third category overlaps with the first two; moreover, the suggested categories do not escape the nature of 'ideal types'. Nevertheless, the classification is operationally convenient since every single use of 'national interest' falls predominantly, though seldom completely, within one of the proposed categories.

On the aspirational level, national interest refers to the vision of the good life, to some ideal set of goals which the state would like to realize if this were possible. If national interest is professed on the aspirational level alone, this means that it is not actively pursued but it does *not* mean that it is politically irrelevant. It still indicates the general direction desired and, given an opportunity through favourable changes in the environment or in capabilities, it may become operational. Thus, while we would be mistaken in attributing an immediate operational significance to the professed Soviet desire to communize the world, we would be likewise mistaken in considering this desire as meaningless and as incapable of becoming operational in some favourable circumstances.

The following points can be made about aspirational interests as distinct from operational ones:

1 They are normally long-term interests;

2 They are generally rooted in history and/or ideology;

3 They command more attention from an opposition free of the restraints of, and the preoccupation with, the tasks of governing than from the actual government. Within political parties they are the major concern of extremist factions which are concerned with ideological purity;[1]

4 Even when they do not directly influence actual policy, they can provide purpose or direction, or at the least, a sense of hope (c.f. pan-Arabism or pan-Africanism, or the messianic ideas in Polish history);

5 They need not be fully articulated and co-ordinated and they can be contradictory;

6 They do not require a 'feasibility study' and are rarely if ever costed;

7 They are determined by political will rather than by capabilities—ideology is a strong determinant. The influence of power is ambivalent: while an ambition may be due to the people's awareness of the power of their state, it can be likewise due to their awareness of their powerlessness and their escape into daydreams, as in the cases above-mentioned under 3.

On the operational level, national interest refers to the sum total of interests and policies actually pursued. Operational interests tend to differ from aspirational ones in respect of the following characteristics:

1 They are usually short-term interests, capable of achievement within the foreseeable future;

2 They often, but not exclusively, stem from considerations of expediency or necessity;

3   They are the predominant concern of the gove...
    ment and/or party in power;

4   They are used in a descriptive rather than a norma-
    tive form.[2]

5   Owing to the practical problems of implementation,
    contradictions among them are less easily tolerated
    than among aspirations;

6   They are generally translated into policies which are
    based upon the assessment of their prospects of suc-
    cess and which can be at least approximately costed;

7   The crucial variable in their determination is found
    in capabilities rather than in political will. Hence
    the hypothesis can be advanced that classification of
    states by power is here more relevant than that by
    ideology. It is likely that all small states, whatever
    their ideology, merely react to overwhelming inter-
    national stimuli; with them policy is distinct from
    positive purpose;

8   They can be systematically arranged into maximum
    and minimum programmes, the former approximat-
    ing aspirational interests. Such arrangement, how-
    ever, depends upon systematic planning of foreign
    policy and rarely, if ever, actually takes place; only
    Soviet foreign policy in some of its aspects can be
    regarded as a reasonable example.

The *interrelationship* between the aspirational and the
operational levels is of great political significance as the distance
between the two levels plays a major part in determining political dynamism.

Dynamism is absent in the two limiting cases: when the aspirations are clearly beyond any chance of achievement and when
they are pitched so low that they merely approximate actual
policies.[3] No convincing examples for these extremes can be

found in reality but they are approximated, on the one hand, by the aspirations of broad international leadership by men such as Sukarno, or Nkrumah, and, on the other, by the very limited conservative international aspirations of a country such as Portugal. A unique and probably unrepeatable case was nineteenth-century Britain at the height of her imperial powers. Although speaking in a mood of exasperation, Lord Salisbury vividly describes his own practice which shows that his aspirations did not reach much further than his actual policies: 'English policy is to float lazily downstream occasionally putting out a diplomatic boat-hook to avoid collisions.'[4]

Changes, whether in the power of the state or in its environment which modify its 'net achievement capability', can seriously affect the distance between aspirations and policies since any revision of the concept of 'national interest' need not take place at the same time at both levels. Thus, when the achievement of some operational goals is blocked repeatedly or over a long period of time, these goals may be either shifted to the aspirational level or dropped altogether. Likewise, when goals are maintained for a long time at the aspirational level without any bearing upon actual behaviour, they may be dropped but their importance may also be enhanced as part of time-honoured tradition.

The inevitable divergence between aspirations and actual policies results in institutional tensions between the central decision makers and those who execute their decisions on the classical 'staff line' pattern. Those responsible for operational definitions of interests tend to arrive at them inductively, by adding up single elements and are greatly concerned with implementation and with costs. Those responsible for the determination of aspirations often think deductively, starting from first principles and ignoring the problems of implementation and of cost. The tasks, moreover, cannot be neatly divided and friction seems inevitable. We find it particularly in Soviet foreign policy in which the conduct of actual operations has come to resemble that in the West but ideological central intervention frequently occurs, creating the impression that some policy decisions may be determined by aspirations alone, without full regard to operational problems. The problem exists, however, also in the West, e.g. in relating general policy papers and specific decisions in the work of the United States National Security Council.[5]

The distinction between the aspirational and the operational levels is, however, only analytical and does not fully occur in real life. Here aspirations and operational interests are frequently, sometimes deliberately, confused, e.g. when in the summer of 1969 Prime Minister Harold Wilson disclaimed the likelihood of a federal Europe within the foreseeable future he may have been talking either about his aspirations or merely stating that his prospective policies would recognize the political actualities in Europe. He may have meant both, although for different publics—to persuade the anti-Europeans in the Labour Party that he is opposed to the federal ideas while demonstrating to the prospective continental associates his appreciation of political reality. In fact these messages could reach the wrong publics and his announcement could be taken on the Continent as a repudiation of an ideal rather than a recognition of reality.

On the *explanatory and polemical* level, in political argument, the concept of 'national interest' is used to explain, evaluate, rationalize or criticize foreign policy. Its main role is to 'prove' oneself right and one's opponents wrong and the arguments are used for this purpose rather than for describing or prescribing. The most important sources are official documents published (white and coloured papers) and statements by heads of government and foreign ministers made in parliament, at press conferences and on other occasions. A special category of these are made for international consumption—diplomatic notes, statements made during foreign visits and in the United Nations. The non-official sources such as parliamentary debates, discussion in the mass media, are also relevant.

Statements vary according to the public addressed and the occasion, both of which determine which single aspects of the national interest are given prominence. Hence contents-analysis of statements requires great caution but changes over a period of time in such dimensions as frequency, length, articulateness, comprehensiveness can be used as partial yardsticks for the definition of the national interest, particularly when they are made by the same incumbent of an office and on similar occasions. Of course, the objective of persuading somebody or of winning an argument alters the relevance of the values common to the aspirational and the operational levels. Tradition, ideology or expediency may be referred to as the most telling arguments and rationalizations rather than as determinants of national interests. Hence differences of opinion between individuals and groups about the nature of national interest tend to be accentuated at this level; arguments and polemics do not necessarily imply fundamental disagreements about the actual aspirations and the operational interests.

There is no necessary correlation between the arguments advanced and the real reasons for which the definition of the national interest is actually arrived at. It may be a case of trying to sell 'the right case' for wrong but most appealing reasons, as well as that of trying to find the 'right' reasons to explain away a 'bad case'; it may be a rationalization—a justification of a traditional practice or of a contingent action based on no firmer basis than a reaction to some environmental stimulus. The critics merely reverse the arguments of the defenders. Political arguments about single issues are often directed to various international and domestic publics each of which requires a different argument so that the same policy can be pleaded for and against in vastly different, sometimes contradictory terms. Quite often people formulate their explanations and rationalizations in order to convince not only others but also themselves about the wisdom of their aspirations and/or policies.

The relationship between declarations and actual aspirations and policies is generally unclear. As no scientific tools exist for its determination, we are reduced to impressionistic guesses and to hunches. Thus Mr. Wilson's denial (mentioned above) of a foreseeable federal future for Europe, may refer to his aspiration or to his proposed policy arrived at on the basis of his estimate of the present situation in Europe, or to some combination of both. Even if he chose to clarify this statement authoritatively himself, we could not be sure whether his argument accurately represented his views or that his views on the subject were constant and clear. Let us consider the recurrent Soviet statements about the inevitable historical process of the world becoming Communist, which, one surmises, implies that the Russians intend to hasten this process. Can we ascertain that these represent aspirations or an actual policy, or some mixture of both? We are baffled although, unfortunately, Soviet intentions are the major independent variable in western defence and foreign policy planning.

It seems advisable to start with the operational level since the interests and policies actually pursued are more concrete than aspirations or arguments; moreover, it is generally easier to find objective criteria for their evaluation. The aspirations can be brought in as an extension of the discussion, mainly in order to ascertain the distance between the two levels. Finally, the explanatory and polemical level is the most prolific source of information; considering it separately should help us to evaluate the arguments employed as possible but not necessarily correct, indicators of the definition of national interest at the other two levels. This scheme has the advantage of being able to accommodate and incorporate the findings of some other approaches. Thus Marxist ideology distinguishes a 'dialectical' juxtaposition of theory and practice which roughly corresponds with that of the aspirational and operational levels. The Marxist distinction is, like the one proposed here, theoretical. In practice it is impossible to find either entirely 'pure' components which would give the individual a unified and conscious world-view or completely 'practical' components which would give him rational instruments for action.[6]

Similarly, Professor M. Seliger, in his examination of the electoral behaviour and of the ideologies of the Israeli political parties, finds a discrepancy between two levels of ideology: the fundamental principles determining the final goals and grand vistas of their realization, and an 'operative ideology', '. . . the argumentation in favour of the policies actually adopted'. He does not, however, distinguish between political argument and political action.[7]

Foreign—domestic distinctions

'National interest' usually refers to foreign policy but is, although less frequently, applied also to domestic politics, e.g. when it is said that it is in the national interest for industry to become more productive or for larger numbers of students to receive mathematical or technological training. When referring to the domestic sphere, we often employ alternative terms, such as 'public' or 'general interest', 'public' or 'social good', etc.

Governments, like Janus, have two faces: they watch and pursue public interests and policies both in the international and the domestic fields. These fields are interconnected and we can think about governmental activities as one complex of inputs and outputs, some of them received from and/or directed to the domestic and the others similarly related to the international environment. We could agree to use national interest in the broader comprehensive meaning, including domestic politics. It seems, however, preferable to confine it to foreign policy, leaving the cognate terms of 'public' or 'general' interest to cover the latter in order to distinguish between domestic and foreign politics.

First, the parameters of action in the two spheres are different. Similar constraints arise from the limitation of resources but, in the domestic sphere, the state has generally sufficient control over the individuals and the subgroups to impose upon them some notion of a general good. In the international sphere, the government comes up against the conflicting wills of other states which often prove inflexible—necessity is here a much harder master.

Second, the basic objectives of foreign and domestic politics differ. Foreign policy centres upon survival and defence. Many of its elements are closely connected with elements of domestic politics, for example foreign trade and defence expenditure have an obvious bearing upon prosperity and the standard of living, but they are considered from quite a different angle.

Third, in domestic politics, it is possible to cast some doubt upon the very existence of common good. For instance, the theory of bargaining, which goes as far back as Aristotle, reduces the notion of public interest to what arises from accommodation among interacting partial interests. By contrast, despite all the difficulties of definition, foreign policy is generally conceived as being based upon the concept of 'national interest' which is deemed to represent the whole society and not to be a mere compromise between partial interests. Further analysis may lead us to a different conclusion but so far even those western critics who refer to national interest as a myth have not denied the crucial significance of its image. Nor, in fact, have Marxist critics done so. To them, national interest represents the interest of the ruling class, which is disguised by the ruling class as being the interest of the people as a whole. Once, however, the people become aware of the hoax, they are supposed to establish a government of their own and thus to turn the myth of national interest into reality.

Fourth, having the monopoly of both diplomacy and defence, the central concerns of foreign policy, governments play a much more exclusive role in its formulation than in domestic politics. The individuals and the subgroups are here generally more ignorant and powerless, and less directly concerned, than within the domestic context. This distinction applies mainly to the West but also in the Communist states (where the party fulfills many of the functions of western governments) social pressures in the field of foreign policy have not been matching the mounting popular pressures about domestic social policy. In new states foreign policy is very remote from the politically unsophisticated people.

In spite of the obvious connection between domestic and foreign policies, for the time being at least, the problems of 'linkage' remain largely unexplored. We cannot, except in impressionistic, general terms, convey the connections in any specific issue. It is even hard to agree which of the policies is primary. On the one hand, systems-analysis offers an attractively simple and plausible explanation in terms of systems disequilibria—that states, like all other systems, try to reduce their domestic disequilibria to the minimum and shape their foreign policies accordingly. On the other hand, it is possible to dwell upon the necessities arising more starkly in the international environment which is more intractable whereas the domestic environment is generally more open to manipulation.

The confusion between 'national' and 'public interest' (or between foreign and domestic politics) may be deliberate or subconscious. When public policy priorities cannot be agreed upon or readily determined, governments frequently take refuge in directing public attention to external pressures, and in stressing the necessity of defence against the dangers (real or imaginary) stemming from the international environment. This expedient is particularly popular with authoritarian regimes. Especially in pluralistic western countries, national interest can serve as a cloak for sectional demands, e.g. to maintain a large defence establishment, to develop a technology with pronounced anti-social aspects (such as supersonic planes), to keep wages down, etc. It is clearly convenient for the vested interests to equate opposition with lack of patriotism or with disloyalty to the nation.

It is often a major element of political controversy whether to concentrate upon the domestic or the foreign sphere. For example in the classical United States debate between the 'realists' and the 'idealists', T. I. Cook and M. Moos[8] came out strongly against the realist concentration upon domestic affairs and claimed that internationalist interests signify no lack of concern for American well-being—their wealth, freedom and culture at home. Similar differences divided the advocates of social welfare who opposed the British involvement east of Suez or the United States involvement in Vietnam.

3/Theories of National Interest

National interest and its components

One of the gravest obstacles to a commonly acceptable definition of national interest is the fundamental disagreement between those who conceive it broadly and hence rather vaguely and those who try to pin it down to a number of concrete single interests, elements, factors, functions or dimensions; all these terms are used without clear distinction in a partly differentiated but mainly overlapping manner.

When we deal with a field as broad and as hard to comprehend as foreign policy, the temptation to resort to generalities becomes overwhelmingly strong. Many claim that any attempt to break down the concept of 'national interest' into its components, or into single interests, is bound to leave out the essentials and also to give scope to the pursuit of sectional interests at the cost of the general good. Even professed pragmatists are not immune to generalizations: Maynard Keynes's comments on the behaviour of economists can be used with even greater justification about politicians: 'Practical men, who believe themselves to be quite exempt from any intellectual influences, are usually the slaves of some defunct theoretician.'[1] The ideas underlying the analytical approach can be best explained by the following breakdown of the concept of 'ownership', proposed by T. E. Weldon: 'the concept of national interest is usually seen as lacking in differentiated content, when it should be seen as containing a number of different functions. N.I. = N.I. should be N.I. = a + b + c + d ... + n, where N.I. is the concept of national interest and a to n are its different functions.'[2]

It is relatively rare for anybody to adopt an extreme position as such a person would have to be fully preoccupied either with a very limited range of interests which narrows his outlook, or with a theory so general that it blinds him to all concrete elements. The emphasis differs from that in domestic politics where the divergence of competing interests is striking and where it is possible to deny the very existence of anything called 'general' or 'public' interest. In foreign policy, it is impossible to deny altogether the existence of a national interest, however vague and nebulous it may appear to be, at least as an important datum. Here, in the absence of similar divergences and clashes between sectional interests, a basic agreement on national interest as a whole is much more readily reached. Furthermore, politicians are attracted by the relative ease of establishing the consensus about foreign policy, and tend to concentrate upon this consensus in order to carry it into the more intractable domestic politics; hence the temptation to use symbolism, to appeal to emotions and overstress the dangers stemming from the international environment.

Normally, national interest is interpreted in a mixed way. Interpretation depends upon several sets of contradictory considerations. First, decisions at the operational level tend to be conceived within a narrow context in which only a few dimensions are considered whereas decisions at the aspirational level as well as explanations and rationalizations refer to national interest as a whole and to the broad principles involved in it. Second, on the operational level the processes of reasoning tend to be inductive; at the other two levels they tend to be more deductive. Thirdly, people with a theoretical, philosophical bias take more interest in the aggregate, whereas those with an empirical, scientific bias put more emphasis upon the single dimensions of the concept. This is an example of the general tendency of contemporary social sciences to break down intractable social problems and concepts into more manageable elements.

Fourth, social roles play a differentiating part. Top level

decision makers (statesmen, prominent politicians, and senior civil servants, especially planners) as well as people not directly involved in government (academics or publicists) generally take more interest in the aggregate. Lower-ranking politicians and civil servants (the executants of policies determined by others) as well as people directly engaged in a particular activity or interest (e.g. exporters of a single commodity, or people with relations, friends, or investments in a foreign country) tend to take a narrower interest in the single elements of national interest. Fifth, powerful ideological beliefs stimulate interest in the aggregate, as shown in the patriotic appeals by the nationalists or in the expositions of the Communist millenium by the Marxists.

Finally, the effect of the power position of the state is ambivalent. A state with limited capabilities is governed mainly by contingencies, is more closely tied to the operational level and is less capable of developing its aspirational interests. Simultaneously, however, the scope[3] of its national interest is much more circumscribed, making it easier for its rulers to comprehend and to pursue this interest as a whole.

Comparative data are available on as many as 230 national attributes of 82 states and correlations between these and the propensity to conflict has been subjected to a searching although so far inconclusive analysis.[4] The method could be further evolved and applied to the definition of national interest: e.g. how is this definition affected by the state possessing a territory much smaller than those of neighbours and rivals? What are the conditions in which the state reacts by trying to expand or to compensate in other elements, or by accepting the territorial deficiency as a restraint? Do any other attributes of states create a tendency to react in one of these ways? Such stock-in-trade problems of international behaviour can be better articulated and can be analysed more systematically and in greater depth.

General theories of politics

Analysis of national interest belongs to the age-long stream of philosophical speculation about the good state and the good society. In the narrower sense, used here (as pertaining to foreign policy), despite its frequent employment, the concept has not played a central part in human thought; only the Americans were sufficiently concerned with the purpose and the meaning of their foreign policy to produce a sizeable literature directly concerned with national interest.[5]

The general literature on moral and political philosophy as well as much of the broadly conceived historical and legal analysis contains some relevant discussion although the references are often indirect and implicit. The most pertinent contributions can be found in the literature dealing with the state or the international system; the analysis of power is also highly relevant in so far as it is related to the purposes for which power is used.

The analysis of the *state* and its *government*[6] is the most important and impressive field of political thought but it is not directly concerned with national interest. Traditionally, scholars have been concentrating upon domestic affairs—the structure of government, the relations between the individual and authority, etc. Such early models as those of a pyramid or a balance, or the more complex ones of mechanism or an organism, gradually adopted from the natural sciences from the end of the Middle Ages, allowed the scholars to analyse the state in isolation from the international environment. Moreover, all these models and theories were concerned with the discovery of certain immutable laws and left no room for the elements of purpose, choice and decision. The latter were introduced only by the historians.

Relevant modern theories and models concerned with human behaviour and with social organization pay due regard to their purposes. Sometimes they directly discuss international behaviour as a sub-category of human behaviour (e.g. Nicholas

Rashevsky included 'interaction among nations' as one of the forms of interaction among social groups). Sometimes their models and theories are applicable only to international behaviour. In some cases they have not yet been fully applied; thus nobody has so far made full use of Herbert Simon's models of 'optimisation' and 'adaptive behaviour', or Max Weber's concept of 'ideal types' as an approach to the study of classical diplomacy evolved in nineteenth-century Western Europe, especially in French and British practices.

The 'structural-functional' analysis developed by Talcott Parsons and Robert K. Merton, could be applied to foreign policy; moreover, in this context, it would escape much of the fundamental weakness of which it is often accused; that it presupposes social goals and purposes but cannot explain how these are established. The basic purposes of foreign policy postulated until recently were found in two interconnected complexes of goals: one centring upon survival, defence, preservation of independence and maintenance of geographical boundaries and another one centring upon diplomacy. These arise from the very fact of existence within the international society.

The basic purpose of foreign policy in the past could be summed up as the maintenance of state sovereignty, a concept which became the foundation of international relations and was inflated into a powerful myth. Undoubtedly, under the impact of the recent changes in the international environment, this sovereignty, never complete in the past, has been eroded and has been to a large and growing extent replaced by the interdependence of states.[7] It is much to the credit of contemporary writers on politics that they have managed to conceptualize these changes, e.g. in terms of boundaries and their maintenance which form a central part of the cybernetical and the systems analysis approaches. The stark and unreal rigidity of geographical boundaries is mitigated when we consider the state not only as an autonomous political system, but also as a subsystem of the international system. The fluid nature of the concept of boundaries is illuminated when we apply it not only to relations among states but also to those within each state, between 'polity' and society. When systems are defined by social communication, patterns of political boundaries are shown merely to reflect and induce and sometimes clash with discontinuities in this communication.

Theories of the *international system* have a different focus from the theories of the state. They are, nevertheless, intimately connected with them as the state has to maintain its sovereignty within the international system and hence is directly affected by the nature of that system.

The most important school of thought in the field is concerned with the 'balance of power' to which many writers attribute a fundamental role in politics. Although many variants have been proposed, the essentials of the approach are simple. Its proponents claim that the international behaviour of states is governed predominantly by power considerations and hence that the operation of the international system imposes as the supreme goal of national interest a power position sufficiently strong to counteract any possible dangers. This can be achieved by improving the capabilities of the state as well as by securing allies, mainly on the principle of 'the bad neighbour policy'. The underlying theory is that clashes of interest are likely to arise with neighbours, and therefore neighbours are destined to be enemies; hence it is a sound principle to form 'natural' alliances with states not sharing a common boundary but being contiguous to a neighbour and likewise hostile to it. This is the gist of the *mandala*, the theory evolved in Mauryan India, but it applies with equal power to Western Europe during the heyday of the 'balance-of-power' system, when the Concert of Europe operated in the nineteenth century.[8]

The balance of power theories did rarely, if ever, indicate a crude maximization of power as the basic goal of national interest. Particularly during the operation of the Concert of Europe both theory and practice favoured only what Herbert

Simon calls in his theory of organization 'satisficing' power requirements. It was not in the interests of a member of the Concert to amass excessive power as this would bring the balance principle into operation and would induce an alliance of others against him. He needed merely as much power as was necessary to deter and, if need be, fend off an attack by others —although, in view of the uncertainty of the calculations and of the risks involved, a fair margin of safety had to be added. All members showed an interest in the preservation and the operation of the international system.

Since 1945 the advent of nuclear power has brought into question the traditional balance of power theory. On the one hand the theory is still operated in the modern form of 'the balance of terror' which applies only to nuclear powers, and in fact only to the two superpowers. This theory prescribes as an imperative goal of national interest the maintenance of a sufficient second-strike nuclear force to deter an attack by the adversary. At the same time, in order to avoid the dangers of escalation, it indicates also an interest in the operation of an international order within which violent conflicts would be circumscribed, going far beyond the concern of the states in the nineteenth century.

A further important theory of the international system is that of 'collective security'. It was incorporated into the Covenant of the League of Nations largely on the basis of President Wilson's ideas, and it was based upon revulsion against power politics and the ineffectiveness of the balance of power, for which it was supposed to act as a substitute. The basic objective of the new approach was to pit the collective power of all 'peace-loving' states against any aggression, by whomever and wherever it might be perpetrated.

With respect to the concept of 'national interest', the balance of power and the collective security theories are fundamentally similar. Both realistically assume that the survival of the state may be endangered by aggressive behaviour of others and that the state must not only maintain its own capabilities but must also contribute to the shaping of a safer international environment. Thus both aim at what Arnold Wolfers calls 'milieu' and not 'possession goals'; both assume that the narrowly defined national interest can be transcended in the direction of internationalism.[9] The important divergence between the two theories lies in the different methods which they adopt for securing a safer world.

Theories of 'national interest' can be distilled from generalizations about the international behaviour of states which has been subjected to much analysis in the last half century, especially by writers concerned with *power politics*. All thinkers concerned with this behaviour are inevitably struck by the fact that a state, while wishing to exert its will and secure its interests, is all the time confronted with other states which wish to exert *their* wills and secure *their* interests. In all ages and in all international systems the wills clash and the interests conflict, periodically leading to wars and to the disappearance of some state units.

In view of the threat to the survival of mankind arising from the continuation of this pattern in the nuclear age, much thought has been devoted to an advance towards a system in which conflict resolution and reconciliation of the wills of the separate states would be achieved without war. Nothing convincing has been proposed; as long as the states remain in separate existence, the clashes of will and of interest are likely to recur. We can improve the methods of conflict resolution, circumscribe the use of force, and foster the awareness of the interdependence of states, but all these are no more than palliatives. A fundamental change can be achieved only by unification under some form of world government and this, all agree, cannot be envisaged in the foreseeable future.

It does not make much difference whether the adherents of the theory of power politics postulate a basic lust for power, an *animus dominandi*, or regard it as a derivative from the anarchic state of international relations. In both cases they tend to draw an analogy between the international system and Hobbes's state of nature in that the units—the states and the individuals respectively—are threatened in their very survival and hence seek security, the only ultimate basis for which is force. This is the foundation of the power theory of national interest which, in its extreme form, equates it with the power necessary for security and survival. In fact, the majority of the proponents of the power theory recognize that the relationship between security and force is much more complex and considerations other than those of power must be taken into account.[10]

In his *War and Peace: a Theory of International Relations*,[11] Raymond Aron discusses the goals of foreign policy in terms which amount to a refined and amended restatement of the power theory. First, he recognizes that the complex relationship between security and force is a major obstacle to a rational optimization of power. Second, following David Hume, he adds the objective of 'glory', of securing the satisfaction of the *amour-propre* of the nation and its esteem by others. This is an important addition as this striving for glory cannot be fully equated with the seeking of prestige which is directly an element of power. For instance in the rivalry between the Americans and the Russians in the exploration of outer space there seems to be also an additional competitive element which can be simply explained as the desire to be there first.

By and large, as power is fundamentally only an instrumentality to achieve other values, its analysis cannot serve as the basis of a full explanation of international behaviour.[12] Consequently we cannot use it as a basis for the definition of national interest although power considerations play in it an extremely important role.

Other general theories of domestic and of international politics are only indirectly relevant. This applies even to theories of nationalism. It does, of course, make a great difference to the moral and metaphysical foundations of national interest whether we postulate the nation as the supreme good or refuse to do so. Writers on nationalism do not, however, shed much light upon this problem as they are primarily concerned with the analysis of the concepts of 'the nation' and of 'nationalism' and about their relevance in history and politics.

By the nature of things, most analyses of politics refer to national interest. They tend, however, to postulate it or to accept it as given in terms of their arguments rather than to analyse it. To take for example the classical concept of 'sovereignty', writers about it assume that states conceive their national interest primarily in the terms of the maintenance of sovereignty. The fashionable social communication approach assumes in its own terms a similar national interest of autonomy in social communication. Neither explains whether the postulated contents of 'national interest' lie in the very nature of our political systems or whether they are defined with some degree of freedom, and if so, in what way.

4/Dimensions of National Interest: I

Some major classifications

The preceding chapter has surveyed the major relevant general theories which offer promising angles of approach and insights into the nature of national interest. This chapter and the next will survey and develop the less ambitious but likewise inconclusive attempts to separate significant and logically coherent categories, aspects and elements. The distinctions made and the classifications derived from them vary in their theoretical accomplishments but all share one limitation: they fail to provide an effective guide to a generally valid orderly arrangement, classification and evaluation of concrete acts of foreign policy. It is relatively easy to agree about the theoretical relevance of the categories proposed but not about their relative importance and, even less so, about the way to co-ordinate them into one coherent logical system.

In theory, the most logical distinction lies between three groups of variables: structural, behavioural and relational. All the possible variables are included in these three classes as each can be logically subsumed under one of these, but difficulties arise from the absence of clear-cut boundaries between them in real life.[1] For instance, when tracing the variables related to the attitudes to international Communism included in the United States' conception of national interest, we cannot avoid dealing with all the three classes of variables: the structure of United States politics, the dynamics of these politics and United States relations with Communist states. Another basic distinction can be made between *cognitive* and *volitional* (or effective) variables, the former related to the image of the world held by the decision makers and the latter to their values. This distinction is analytically important but, again, we must invariably take botn. classes into account when dealing with any aspect of national interest in real life.

Real life does not readily yield to the logic of these clear-cut distinctions or to any other ones. While it is a mistake to try to force reality into the strait-jacket of a conceptual scheme, each scheme can be helpful in the sorting out of some ambiguities and uncertainties of a specific situation; in fact, several schemes can be used simultaneously or consecutively, provided their limited role is fully appreciated.

Raymond Aron[2] proposes a distinction according to the objects to which the goals of foreign policy refer: space, men, and souls. This corresponds with the generally accepted importance attributed in all analyses of international politics to the geographical, the demographic and the ideological elements. This classification is complete as all the goals can be related to one of the three elements: in theory, a simple choice lies between either extending the territory of the state or the numbers of people under its sway or ensuring the triumph of its ideas. Although in practice these objectives are hard to separate, the distinction is analytically important as it draws our attention to the possibility of substituting one class of objectives for another and hence broadens the area of our choice.

A similar claim can be made for a distinction proposed by Arnold Wolfers[3] into 'possession goals' and 'milieu goals', according to whether they refer to the domestic or the international environment. This is an analytical category particularly useful for sloughing off the crudities of the power theory because it enables us to group separately the elements relating to the state in its aspects as a relatively autonomous sovereign unit engaged in power relations, and those relating to it as an interdependent subunit of the international system.

A general distinction should be drawn between *independent* foreign policy goals (ends) and *dependent* goals (means).[4] The ends/means relationship helps us to rank goals and offers another corrective to the crude power political approach by enabling us to look at power as a dependent goal, i.e. in relation to the objectives it purports to serve.

Since national interest is determined in the physical world, all its elements must be in some way related to the two fundamental dimensions of this world, those of *space* and of *time*. How relevant these dimensions are is best shown by the recurrent grave blunders committed in the conduct of foreign policy because the formula of national interest arrived at in a specific context of space and time is applied to situations with a different context.

Strategy, politics and economics

One of the most frequently employed divisions is that into strategic, political and economic dimensions. This distinction, which corresponds with the customary division of governmental tasks between separate ministries, has been frequently and rightly attacked for its tendency to lead to three distinctly conceived policies. These separate policies being formulated and pursued in their individual contexts and insufficiently co-ordinated, do not serve and often even damage the national interest conceived as a whole. Nevertheless, regardless of departmental divisions and co-ordination, governmental activities in foreign policy fall within the three fairly well defined categories of strategic/military, political/diplomatic, and economic, each of which requires a different expertise. Hence, the administrative division and the distinction of three corresponding dimensions within the national interest are both fully warranted. The difficult administrative problems of co-ordinating separate agencies, so well documented in the United States' foreign policy, are fully matched by the intellectual problems of co-ordinating the corresponding three dimensions of national interest which starkly appear in the recurrent debates about defence and economics. Subsequent paragraphs merely outline the intractable problems of this intellectual co-ordination, without trying to resolve them.

Although no clear models of a rational foreign policy to be aspired to have been proposed either by statesmen or by their analysts and critics, the basic pattern implied in most statements and writings on the subject is reasonably similar and simple: the national goals are politically determined, the strategic goals should serve them, the country's economy has to supply the wherewithal and hence economic considerations serve as a source of means as well as a constraint. The balance between the three dimensions has always been delicate— political goals can readily impose strategic ones which are beyond the military potential and/or the economic resources of the state; strategic goals through their own momentum may pervert political goals as well as impose unbearable economic burdens; economic goals competing with the costs of strategy can cripple the state's military arm and upset its foreign policy. History abounds in examples for each category of problems.

As in other social issues involving the reconciliation of opposed considerations, it is possible to conceive of periodical rhythmic changes in emphasis in the form of the swing of the pendulum. Concern with military goals endangers expenditure which eventually grows beyond what is politically acceptable; a reaction sets in which gradually curtails military expenditure to the point of jeopardizing the country's political goals and security and the pendulum swings back again. Professor Nilson made a close study of these fluctuations in the reign of Queen Anne during which they were connected with the alternations between the Whigs and the Tories, and found a close parallel to what the economists call the 'cobweb theorem' of the fluctuations in the price of agricultural commodities: high prices lead to increasing supplies, these in turn lead to the lowering of prices which eventually leads to the shrinking of supplies and to a consequent upward swing of prices; then the circle repeats itself.[5] Apparently social systems follow the pattern of biological ones in reconciling dichotomous tasks and conflicting tendencies.

They generally avoid a fixed solution and limit themselves to prescribing tolerable parameters; the constant fluctuations can occasionally become disturbing but ensure the desirable flexibility.

Since the War military costs have escalated so much that the problem of reconciling economic and other dimensions has become different in kind. Moreover, whereas we have made great progress in analysing and estimating the costs of various activities and institutions in terms of money and are making some progress even with putting into monetary terms their social costs, no parallel progress has been made in quantifying benefits. For instance, the costs of economic aid are fairly clear but how does one measure any ensuing influence on the recipient and, furthermore, put it into cash terms? The difficulties arising from our attempts to extend quantification from the economic to the other dimensions of foreign policy can be illustrated by the example of post-war United States. There the application of economic methods of cost-effectiveness to defence expenditure under Robert MacNamara has not been very successful and, in all likelihood, the misleading concentration-quantification contributed to the disastrous escalation of the United States involvement in Vietnam. The Planning, Programming and Budgeting (PPB) system is now out of favour as a panacea; characteristically it was never applied to the Department of State.

The salience* of the economic dimension of national interest greatly differs. This is fairly obvious and to be expected when one compares the foreign policies of different states. Thus, in the relations between the western states and the Soviet Union, the former have generally given priority to economics and to trade whereas the latter has been always more concerned with the political and strategic dimensions. Among the western

* In this context 'salience' can be approximately defined as something of immediate importance. For fuller discussion of the term see following section, pp. 61–67.

states, great differences have arisen between Britain and the United States over the politically desirable interdiction of strategic supplies to Communist countries—while Britain accords a priority to economic considerations, the United States accords it to strategic and political ones.

Even within the foreign policy of a single country the salience of the economic dimension fluctuates in time. In post-war Britain, for instance, the tug of war between guns and butter, the see-saw between a sound economy and a more adequate defence, have created acute tensions with the disturbing result that the greatest defence effort, following the outbreak of the Korean War in 1950, was made when the country could least afford it whereas in later defence efforts economies were made when the country's defence problems had become more acute.[6] The recurrent currency crises and economic stagnation eventually led to a violent swing in favour of economics. Especially since the decision to withdraw from east of Suez in 1967, the growing salience of economics has become increasingly reflected in national policy.

Although it is generally hard to estimate the changes in the salience of economic considerations, the factors involved appear to be relatively clear and simple. In wartime, the strategic dimension is naturally dominant as survival hinges upon military efforts, but only when faced with the danger of defeat in all-out war do states ignore economic restraints altogether and go to the limits of their capacity, as shown by the war efforts of the major European belligerents in the last war. Beyond wars we are confronted with a whole spectrum of situations ranging from those in which an acute danger is perceived—e.g. at the height of the 'Cold War' during the Korean crisis, to really low international tensions. There seems to be an unequivocal correlation between the perception of strategic dangers and the predominance of the strategic dimension at the cost of the economic one.

Traditionally, western states attach much greater importance to matters of trade and economics in their international behaviour than do Communist or new states. When comparing the Soviet Union and the United States in the post-war period, it is clear that the military expenditure required for the present strategic needs of a superpower weighs much more heavily on the less developed Soviet economy which, moreover, cannot successfully satisfy the rapidly growing consumers' demands. The United States' economy is sufficiently strong to carry the full burden of defence expenditure without encroaching on consumption; in fact, it is arguable that the military expenditure is an essential factor in the economy's continuing growth. The rapid escalation of costs of the Vietnam involvement has, however, recently led to growing conviction on the part of the government's critics that the resources thus spent preclude sufficient expenditure on social progress at home. By 1969 a swing towards a greater salience of economics had become prominent whereas the present acute phase in the Soviet conflict with China precludes a similar development in the Soviet Union.

In the 1950s and early 1960s new states appeared to be mainly concerned with their independence to the point of giving full priority to political over economic objectives, sometimes, in the eyes of the more economically-minded western observers, cutting off their noses to spite their faces. A good example can be found in the foreign policy of Indonesia which severely upset Indonesia's economy by severing all ties with the Netherlands after their independence and then by refusing United States aid. This priority accorded to politics militated against the fact that in a world which is generally economically interdependent, new states are economically very much more dependent on others than their more powerful and better established counterparts. They rely on foreign aid and also on foreign markets, a dependence accentuated when, as often is the case, their exports consist mainly of one commodity and/or are directed to one major customer. In the later 1960s some new states at least began to put greater emphasis upon the economic dimension of the national interest. This is pronounced in the foreign policy of Singapore, a new state which, being fully dependent upon trade, clearly accords priority to economics. Singapore limits her political and strategic interests to her immediate environment and divides the remainder of the world into potential trade-partners, investors and aid-givers and others to whom she can remain fairly indifferent.

So far, the argument has dealt with the political and strategic dimensions in an undifferentiated form, opposing them to the economic one. In fact similar problems arise when deciding upon the salience of politics and strategy, the relationship between which is equally intricate. The traditional British idea was that adequate military forces and alliances should, as far as possible, ultimately back both the defence of the realm and the preservation of vital interests abroad. In view of her contracting capabilities, Britain has now greatly reduced the scope of her overseas interests and, especially in South East·Asia, she has now to shift nearly entirely from strategy to politics: as it has been put, she will now need a Foreign Office and not, as hitherto, a Ministry of Defence policy.[7] Only the two superpowers can possibly think about their interests in terms of a reasonable strategic protection and even they have been rapidly shifting their emphasis from it to political means. Small states commanding, by necessity, limited military resources, never had the means to rely fully upon strategy. Outstanding in this respect are the new African states which, being relatively free from the dangers of foreign aggression, tend to concentrate entirely upon the political dimension. The limitation of this policy is clearly shown by their powerlessness to do anything about the racial policies in southern Africa which they all deplore.

The relations between the three dimensions are often bedevilled by dichotomies. Fortunate are the countries in which the political and the strategic dimensions coincide, as in the

Atlantic alignment of Norway and, in the minds of the anti-Europeans, also of Great Britain. It is extremely difficult in the case of Denmark. As an old saying in Danish foreign policy has it, politically the country belongs to Scandinavia but strategically to the Continent; moreover, economically she belongs to both.

The frustrations and satisfactions within the different dimensions of national interest are not easy to estimate. To take examples from the last war on which we have some historical perspective, Norway managed to balance conflicting German and British economic demands, but could not compromise on the British strategic demands for the right of passage of troops for Finland or for action in the Leads. Turkey, which was somewhat less exposed, managed to remain neutral by offering the Germans psychological satisfaction through friendly statements which were to serve as a compensation for the limited economic concessions they made to the British. The latter served as a compensation for refusing Britain's political and strategic demands to join the United Nations against Germany.[8] An interesting case which well illustrates the fluctuating place of the various dimensions is that of Franco-German relations since the Second World War. Whereas in the initial stage the Germans accorded the French numerous far-reaching economic concessions in order to secure their political support, during the November 1968 crisis of the franc they used their economic dominance to resume a more independent political role.

The preceding classification into strategic, political and economic dimensions, corresponds with Raymond Aron's[9] two referents of space and men. His third referent, human souls, is generally distinguished as the ideological dimension of national interest. This dimension embraces all non-material aspects of the concept and can be divided into subcategories related to the political ideology pursued, nationalism, race, culture and religion.

Somewhat related is another persuasive distinction between

material (physical) dimensions which include the physical capabilities possessed and the restraints encountered, and non-material (volitional) elements which include the non-material counterparts to the former as well as elements related to political will, especially ideology.

Salience

'Salience' is a term which has not been fully assimilated in common usage. It is used here because it serves best to convey the joint qualities of importance, prominence, urgency and intensity while, as explained later, it does not fully coincide with any of them. Since the concept has a general bearing upon the formulation of national interest, it is discussed here both in relation to elements and in general terms.

Salience is a compound notion. It can be regarded as roughly equivalent to the *immediate importance* attributed to an issue or element; possible future changes in importance are often so heavily discounted that we must think of salience as characteristic of a short-term view, and hence as potentially clashing with long-range considerations.

Salience can be equated with the *prominence* of the issue, which may coincide with its intrinsic importance but also merely with its sensational news-value. Because it coincides with prominence it sometimes deviates from *urgency* because not all urgent things become prominent and not all prominent things are urgent. Finally, owing to all these considerations, it cannot fully coincide with the *intensity* of a person's attitude although the latter is one of its most important ingredients.

It is harder to agree about the salience of any elements of national interest than about their relevance or any other of their qualities. This fact is generally acknowledged as being of utmost political importance because salience largely determines the choice of priorities. It is not a constant, objectively assessable quality. Its assessment fluctuates so much from person to person and from occasion to occasion that many despair of the possibility of a rational decision about national interest. The problems of comparison are further bedevilled by the uncertainties of simultaneously assessing several states in which calculations must be added up or multiplied by some co-efficient.

Ultimately, salience is determined by the general approach to foreign policy which is governed by a combination of many factors. Specifically one may hypothesize that its assessment depends upon:

1 The scope[10] of the national interest which, in turn, largely depends upon the power status. Small states justifiably complain that what appears to them as salient (and vital) is often deemed much less so by the great powers to whom they are allied. Thus the Poles were most unhappy about Churchill's wartime refusal to press Stalin to agree to the restoration of the pre-1939 Soviet-Polish frontier, as were the Israelis about the United States and Britain not sharing their view of the Egyptian occupation of the Straits of Tiran in 1967.

2 The stress laid either upon domestic or upon international elements. This is the foundation of the most articulate debate on national interest ever held, that between the 'realists' and the 'idealists' in the United States. It is also a major, though seldom fully recognized reason for Britain's failure to exercise her opportunities for leadership in Western Europe after 1945; she was preoccupied with domestic issues such as the establishment of the welfare state and nationalization, and with imperial matters which lie in between the domestic and the foreign fields. The situation in many new states is reversed. Here internationally ambitious leaders, such as Sukarno of Indonesia or Nkrumah of Ghana, pursued their foreign priorities to the neglect of domestic issues.

3 Assessment of relevance which is frequently governed by ideology and considerations of principle rather than by rational calculation of interests. Western observers repeatedly comment on Communist and new states neglecting their 'true', i.e. mainly economic and political interests, for ideological reasons.

In 1969 Mr. Luns, the Netherlands foreign minister for seventeen years, similarly, in retrospect, assessed the way the Dutch had handled the West Irian issue which, he said, was peripheral to their interests but central to their principles. The United States in Vietnam is another example.

4 Tradition based upon historical experience. Although the qualities of importance and urgency can be and sometimes are assessed on the basis of a rational evaluation, tradition often prevails, especially when the situation is unclear and/or time is pressing. Thus while unemployment is the major economic trauma in Britain, money inflation is more salient in Germany; Communism is the bogey in the United States; every state has its traditional favourite allies and adversaries, styles of diplomatic behaviour and of strategy, etc. All these play a significant part in decisions concerning the salience of individual issues.

The intricate relationship between the elements of evaluation is demonstrated by the swings of the pendulum between short- and long-term strategic and economic considerations in Britain's post-war defence policy. The salient ones always won; immediately after the war Britain was so preoccupied with the strategic issues that she assumed a great variety of conventional and nuclear, European and world-wide commitments; when economic stringency prevailed in 1947–48 she shed some of them; following the Korean War, however, the crash rearmament programme was rapidly raised from £3,400 million to £4,700 million in three years and was to a large extent fulfilled despite the lingering basic weakness of the economy; in 1967 economic stringency again prevailed, resulting in the drastic hastening of the withdrawal from east of Suez. In all these cases long-term considerations were invariably heavily discounted.

Once a problem or an element of national interest becomes salient, it is subjected to discussion either by the general public or by some élite, and political forces divide on it before any decision is taken. While an issue must become salient before it is heeded, this does not ensure any particular action, solution or treatment; an issue may remain unresolved even though it has been extensively considered, e.g. the problems of formulating a policy towards Nazism were undoubtedly salient in the later 1930s both in Britain and in France but this did not lead to a firm decision.

In extreme situations, as when war breaks out, salience is inescapably dictated by the importance and urgency of the issues arising; thus, the military/strategic elements were imperiously salient for the Poles, when attacked by Hitler, but much less so for their allies. In less extreme situations, an overwhelming threat may dictate the salience of a problem or of its specific aspects but the evidence can be questioned and the salience disputed. Sometimes a national consensus arises, for instance in the post-1945 period, regarding the mutual fears of the two superpowers at the height of the Cold War, or regarding the Polish and Czechoslovak apprehensions of German reunification and rearmament. Sometimes there is disagreement followed by indecisive action or no action at all, as during the period of appeasement in the 1930s.

When a policy gives some promise of becoming a panacea, all its elements tend to become salient. Prominent examples can be found in the waves of support for international organization in its various phases: the League of Nations and collective security; NATO as an instrument of successful containment; the European communities as a cure for Europe's economic and political troubles. The positive attraction of such policies is generally preceded by and based upon a negative experience as serious disappointment with other important policies. In these three cases, this crucial disappointment had been experienced with the balance of power system, with the aftermath of the 'strange alliance' of wartime, and with the prospects of economic and political revival by individual state effort which arose on the Continent immediately after the war and, in the United Kingdom, only in the 1960s.

In small states, national interest is frequently reduced to the central question of survival. Hence there is less controversy over salience and priorities,[11] especially if the state adjoins a powerful and expansionist neighbour.

When the situation is less acute, in liberal-democratic societies, the salience of issues and elements emerges from the interplay between sectional interests which, ever since Aristotle, has been regarded as the major process of politics. It can be attributed also to the manipulation of public opinion by the power élite through the mass media.[12] Undoubtedly, particularly in the United States, the press gives certain issues and certain dimensions of the national interest much greater prominence than they would otherwise attain and hence makes them salient.[13] An autocratic regime and undeveloped mass media tend to lodge the power of determining the salience of the various elements of the national interest in the hands of the ruling élite. This does not prevent the creation of 'pseudo-events' and arbitrary misjudgements as egregious as those engendered by the manipulation of the mass media by the vested interest in the West.

Independently of the influences and motivations involved, all evaluations of salience fluctuate. A prudent decision-maker endeavours to take into account all important dimensions, irrespective of those immediately urgent. Although the weight to be attached to each cannot be determined in advance, it is possible to prepare a checklist with some weighting or ranking before the stress has arisen and our balance of judgement has been affected by what is immediately urgent. Thus British policy towards Singapore combines the issues of a military base, of an ex-colony to be protected, of Malaysian race politics, and of British policy towards China. If all of these are roughly evaluated and the general evaluation checked with that arrived at when a particular crisis enhances the salience of one of these issues, there is less chance for short-term considerations to affect long-term policies.

3

Whenever two policies, issues or elements are of roughly equal importance but incompatible, obviously the choice of the one inevitably spells neglect of its opposite; the more salient one of them becomes, the more is the other one obliterated. The above mentioned oscillations between strategic and economic priorities in British defence policy provide an example. Likewise during the early period of her post-war rehabilitation, Western Germany was faced with two major tasks: to be fully accepted into international society, and to prepare the conditions for German unification. Theoretically these tasks were not inevitably dichotomous; in practice, German rehabilitation could be best achieved through full integration in the Western world whereas progress towards reunification demanded the support of the Soviet Union which such integration precluded. Thus, when successfully steering his country in the first direction, Dr Adenauer was forfeiting the chances of reunification, although this became clear only gradually.

To take another example, the Warsaw Pact members insist on the removal of United States troops from Germany although their presence prevents the dreaded increased rearmament and full political emancipation of the Federal Republic of Germany; and also provides the Soviet Union with a plausible justification for stationing troops and for intervening in Eastern Europe. Likewise, the repeatedly condemned American intervention in Vietnam served Soviet purposes by creating a diversion along China's border, by reducing United States interest in Europe, and by weakening the political solidarity of NATO; it was useful also to the Chinese by diverting the United States from the vital centres in the north, Taiwan and Okinawa. The closure of the Suez Canal is advantageous for the United States because it prevents the Russians from supplying North Vietnam with heavy military equipment, and from having direct access to the Persian Gulf and the Indian Ocean. Other examples could be added indefinitely. When fundamental incompatibilities are involved, one often wonders whether the salience accorded in political argument corresponds with salience at the operational level; its congruence with that at the aspirational level is even more doubtful.

Finally, what are the possibilities of an empirical investigation of this dimension? Some conventional tools of the social sciences used to inquire into attitudes can be readily applied. For instance it may be possible to administer a questionnaire about some dimensions of national interest to a group of persons active in the field of foreign policy, asking them to rank their opinions and/or to scale them. Correlations between social groups within a national sample and cross-national comparisons can be made. The identical sample may be used for repeating the test in conditions of stress which, by increasing the salience of some elements, enable us to analyse the shifts in the intensity of other elements and provide the material for some understanding of the dynamics of evaluation.

Simulation can be used to check the validity of individual ranking; the individual involved can be subjected to stress by forcing him to take a series of decisions under increasing pressure of time. The order in which he drops the tasks to purchase time for those he deems more salient, provides a reliable index to his priorities.

Scope

As with most aspects of national interest, its scope is determined either by environmental influences, or by volitional acts; as a rule by a combination of the two. Thus the Himalayan states have been forced by international events to abandon isolationism and to enlarge the scope of their national interests, but it was Castro's act of will to enlarge the scope of Cuba's national interest. Franklin Roosevelt's abandonment of isolationism and involvement of the United States in the Second World War is generally interpreted as due to circumstantial influences, i.e. to the rise of totalitarianism and to Japanese expansionism; some American historians, however, attribute it to his deliberate and voluntary act of will. The rise of the United States and Soviet interest in the Third World can be regarded as a mixed case. It was partly due to the establishment of weak independent states which created a potentially dangerous power vacuum, and partly from deliberately conceived designs to intervene in them for ideological, economic, and also humanitarian reasons.

One of the most important variables in determining scope is the relative stress put upon the domestic and the foreign sectors and the following hypothesis can be advanced in this respect. Choices are determined by the comparison of what can be termed 'net achievement capability' in each sector—which can be estimated by confronting the relevant goals, capabilities and constraints. If this 'net achievement capability' is satisfactory in the domestic sector and costs are not unacceptably high, it is prudent to give it preference because domestic processes are more calculable, reliable and manageable. This is the rational basis of the policy of isolationism or near-isolationism. Such policies in a pronounced form are impossible today but the preference for the domestic sector remains marked. States extend their international interests reluctantly, only when they think that such an extension is directly or indirectly beneficial or inevitable. All attempts at internationalization invariably encounter the traditional preference of states to satisfy their goals at home.

The habitual western reasoning is based upon economic rationality; it should pay the government to enlarge the scope of its national interest through shifting elements from the domestic sector to the international sector. But in fact, such economic rationality fails to explain some behaviour in the past, as that of Louis XIV, Napoleon or Hitler, all of whom sought national aggrandizement and glory even at an exorbitant economic cost. It is even less adequate in application to the new states whose rulers, e.g. Sukarno or Nkrumah, are less amenable to it than to the glory-seeking patterns. Communist powers tend to give precedence to ideological and political goals over economic ones. The fact, however, that some international behaviour is not explicable in terms of economic rationality does not invalidate the broader criterion of the 'net achievement capability' here advanced that, whenever the goals of a state cannot be satisfied at home, or can be satisfied only at a high cost, its rulers endeavours to pursue them abroad.

Another important variable is found in the *capabilities* (or elements of power) and the associated *power status* of the country. States can be arranged in broad spectrum at the one end of which we find very weak states which have only a few interests which they can pursue and defend and, at the other, great powers which have few interests which they are not ready to pursue and defend. The greater the capabilities and the higher the power status, the broader the scope of the national interest. This applies primarily to the geographical dimension. Thus the boundaries of the scope of Nigeria's or Ghana's interest cannot be conceived as confined to the African continent as can the interests of their smaller and less powerful neighbours. Moreover, within any given geographical extent the range of the strategic, political and economic interests of the United States is very much broader than that of Argentina, and the range of Argentina, in turn, is broader than that of Bolivia. At present the relevance of capabilities is to some extent diminishing as nuclear deterrence puts major constraints upon the superpowers whereas the working of the international system accords unprecedented protection to small and weak states.

To take some examples, in the post-war years there developed a national consensus in the United States that 'the USA must actively pursue its national interests in the world beyond its boundaries if the Americans are to enjoy the fruits of freedom and prosperity at home.[14] This led to a global interpretation of the scope of the national interest, in which any development, anywhere, was deemed as affecting these interests. This global scope has remained intact as far as the potential relevance of events is concerned but the Americans have drastically revised their views about how active they need to be about the more peripheral interests. With the Communist victory in the autumn of 1949 they withdrew from activities in mainland China; they did not pursue the liberation policy in Eastern Europe announced by President Eisenhower after his election in 1950; chastised by the experiences in Vietnam, they have now decided to curtail their involvement in South-East Asia. The opposite case of the broadening of the scope of the national interest imposed by circumstances can be illustrated by the foreign policies of many new states which, despite their original intentions of remaining non-aligned and uninvolved in the Cold War, have been gradually drawn into the rivalries of the superpowers.

A discrepancy between the capabilities and the power status of a state generally leads to a redefinition of the scope of its national interest but, as a rule, with some time-lag. An example can be found in the contrasting post-war developments in Britain and in Germany or Japan. While Britain started as one of the Big Three but gradually lost her power status and eventually, by 1967, decided to withdraw from east of Suez and to adopt a predominantly regional, Western European orientation, the two defeated powers gradually built up their power status on the foundations of powerful economies and enlarged the scope of their national interests which, as a result of their defeat, had been at first severely restricted. Their capabilities were rapidly built up for three reasons which explain also Britain's continuous economic plight: they were freed from costly overseas commitments; owing to the failure of military adventures, they felt free to concentrate on their economic development; their partially dependent status meant freedom from defence burdens and gave them a momentum of economic growth as well as entitling them to concessions from others.[15] Germany in the late 1950s and Japan in the mid-1960s began to redefine the scope of their interests. De Gaulle's Fifth Republic was a fascinating example of a deliberate enlargement of the scope of interests of a middle power which had suffered great humiliation in wartime and had lost its empire despite prolonged and costly efforts to retain control of it.

Small states tend to limit the scope of their national interest to their more immediate environment and their foreign policy is concerned with a much narrower range of problems and topics.[16] The extreme is a policy aiming at the maximum attainable isolationism. This was historically attempted not only by great powers capable of being more or less self-sufficient but also by small states incapable of actively pursuing their goals abroad. The early wartime motto of the Swedes and the Norwegians was 'the best foreign policy is no foreign policy'. This failed in the case of the Norwegians but was partially successful with the Swedes.[17]

In most cases a full withdrawal is impossible. As noted already by Machiavelli:

> Nor will it do for him to say, 'I do not care for anything' 'I desire neither honour nor profit' 'all I want is to live quietly and without trouble'—for such excuses would not be admitted. Men of condition cannot choose their way of living, and even if they did choose it sincerely and without ambition, they would not be believed; and were they to attempt to adhere to it, they would not be allowed to do so by others.[18]

The impact of capabilities and of power status is greatly modified by the volitional elements which differ enormously from case to case. Thus Fidel Castro deliberately decided to broaden Cuba's national interest which has become in some significant respects much more extensive than that of considerably more powerful Latin American neighbours. He, as well as the leaders of many other small states, pursues goals which are well beyond his capacity to achieve, but even leaders who fully accept the limitation of their capabilities at the operational level remain fully free to determine the scope of their national interest at the aspirational level. Political will depends not only upon the values pursued but also upon the decision maker's image of the environment. Here his span of attention can, to a large extent, determine the scope of the national interest as defined by him. For instance, in contrast to his predecessor, President Johnson was said to be a 'one-crisis man'; he was completely pre-occupied by Vietnam to the point of neglecting other issues and only under the fire of criticism in mid-1956 did he give directions for a large high-power team to broaden his perspectives.[19] Kennedy had been the opposite.

The rapidly growing extent and volume of the activities of all states inevitably broaden the scope of their national interests but the dynamics of the situation may now be changing its direction. At whichever level a state may be, it is no longer interested merely in preserving the *status quo* but aspires to constant growth —of economic production, of standards of living, of social welfare. Much of this expansion can be satisfied only internationally and this cannot fail to broaden the scope of its national interests. Although the areas of social activity are continuing to grow further, for some of them the state is becoming increasingly less suited as the most appropriate form of social organization and sometimes international institutions appear to offer a greater likelihood of effectiveness and success. It is difficult to envisage how the notion of 'national interest' will become reconciled with this evolution[20] and it is conceivable that ultimately its scope will become seriously curtailed.

Another dynamic element rapidly increasing the international involvement of all states is found in the growth of technology which is rapidly reducing social distances by making transport much faster and cheaper. Better facilities for exchanges of goods result in economic integration, better facilities for the use of violence in a broader sphere lead to strategic integration. Until recently it was possible to dispute Machiavelli's denial that a full withdrawal from international affairs is feasible; it is scarcely possible to envisage it now.

5/Dimensions of National Interest: II

The preceding chapter dealt with the various schemes for classifying the dimensions of national interest and with the broad concepts of 'salience' and 'scope'. It would be convenient if now one scheme, whether out of those already advanced or a new one, could be applied in the analysis of the actual dimensions distinguished here. Unfortunately the field of inquiry is too broad and the state of the art too poor to allow for this. Any scheme, however comprehensive for some purposes and in relation to some states, must be found wanting in other contexts. Advance in this direction must be slow and arduous and the best prospects for its progress lie in attempting comparisons of pairs or of small groups of fairly similar or closely interacting states.

The objective of this chapter is therefore limited to three additional fundamental categories which are likely to prove useful in all detailed inquiries and which have not been sufficiently developed in the existing schemes. These are the notion of 'vital' interests, and the spatial and the time dimensions.

Vital interests

No generally accepted criteria exist for defining any interests as vital although all states regard certain interests centring upon national survival as such. Of these, the preservation of the 'vital core' or the 'nerve centre' of the country is most important; interests tend to lose importance with their distance and their lack of connection with this centre.

The traditional hallmark of an interest which is deemed vital is that the state is unwilling to make concessions on it and that it is prepared, if necessary, to go to war over it. The readiness of the nuclear powers to retaliate with a nuclear attack which is obviously circumscribed, is clear only in the case of a direct nuclear threat to the 'vital core'. The fundamental issue of the 'credibility' of the deterrent can be described as that of convincing the adversary that also some other less central interests may be considered sufficiently vital to warrant nuclear retaliation, if they are infringed. All states face similar problems wherever, in accordance with their individual value systems, they regard as vital also interests which have no direct bearing upon national survival.

To enhance the status of interests which are considered vital, they are often represented as being also permanent. In fact their life span is rarely very long as they cannot remain in existence without major alterations once the value-system and/or the 'net achievement capability' has undergone serious changes. Thus the famous Monroe Doctrine has several times altered its meaning since its pronouncement in 1823 but at least its underlying principle has remained; its much more ephemeral successor, the so-called 'British Monroe Doctrine' of 1928, which was commonly understood to apply mainly to the Middle East, has now completely disintegrated. In many cases, such as that of the alleged Russian drive towards warm water ports, historians disagree in interpreting the evidence.

Dramatic changes occur in the imperial interests of states which are deemed vital in one generation but soon go into oblivion. Thus in the sixteenth century Britain gave up her three-centuries-long designs to dominate the Continent and since 1945 she has given up her empire; in the seventeenth century the Swedes abandoned their Baltic empire. Global 'security interests' acquired by originally isolationist states, Britain and the United States, do not remain permanently vital; Britain has abandoned hers while the United States is now in the process of drastic revision. Even attachment to the integrity of the state's territory is not sacrosanct. The Germans have now apparently become fully reconciled to the loss of Alsace-Lorraine and the

Poles no longer aspire to a 'Great Poland' stretching from the Baltic to the Black Sea and have even reluctantly accepted the westward shift of the state's boundaries imposed upon them by the Russians.

The adjective 'vital' added to an interest has an emotional appeal and, as it lacks clear legal or political definition, it is open to abuse in political argument similar to that to which 'national interest' in general is subjected. This happened in the protracted debate about the American involvement in Vietnam. As late as in 1957, when Congress authorized President Eisenhower to protect the 'vital interests' of the United States in the Middle East, the president was not satisfied with this justification; he actually sent 14,000 soldiers to Lebanon but explained this action by the more specific purpose 'to protect American lives and property'. Within a decade, reference to unspecified 'vital' United States interests in Vietnam was made so often as to deprive the term of any real meaning;[1] inevitably reaction to the abuse set in.

Estimates of the 'vital' nature of an interest change under the impact of one of the following factors, or of their combination. First, a change in the values held by the leadership or by the people, or by both; an interest of no great intrinsic importance may become 'vital' when it assumes a symbolic value and/or when it involves national prestige, e.g. redress for a trivial violation of the frontier, or for insult to the national flag. Second, in the definition of interests as 'vital', the capabilities required to secure them, and the estimated cost, must be taken into account. In the contemporary international system the state's most vital interest in preserving its territorial integrity and political independence is in most cases ensured by the stability of the international system but the costs of pursuing interests which are deemed 'vital' and require intervention, are rapidly escalating. As shown by the case of Vietnam, the more remote the involvement, the greater the likelihood that the rising cost will weaken the will of both the people and their leaders, and will eventually lead to defeat. Indeed, the Vietnam case may be considered as a demonstration of a cycle:

> Capability extends vital interests by a process which is inherently self-destructive: each successive extension can be promoted only by further extension, and the cost of each successive extension is higher than the previous one. At some point the cost must exhaust capability, and the process of extension is necessarily halted, and the widespread structure begins to crumble.[2]

When an interest is infringed by another state, the judgement as to how vital this interest is partly depends upon the identity and nature of the infringing state. One crucial variable is the power status of the offending state. A small Central American republic is likely to consider the issue of violation of its frontiers by a similar small neighbour as less vital than one by the United States, provided this neighbour is not a traditional arch-enemy. Another crucial variable is the general nature of relations with the culprit state. Here attitudes are ambivalent. On the one hand, there is a general presumption that friends can do no harm and that one should always put the best possible construction upon their actions. On the other hand, higher standards of behaviour can be expected from a friend than from an unfriendly or hostile state.

Traditionally interests are defined as vital mainly in the strategic/political sphere and are connected with the notion of the power deemed necessary for national survival and for the attainment of many national goals. Since the Second World War not only economic but also psychological and ideological elements have been steadily gaining in importance but the centre of gravity has not decisively shifted in their direction.

The spatial dimension

Space, as Kant has convincingly argued, is fundamental to all thinking which relates to human experience. Any discussion of foreign policy inevitably includes some analysis of space. It is a geographical dimension of international politics; one of the main elements of the state, especially the area it occupies and its boundaries; an element of power; a traditional objective of foreign policy, in its relation to warfare, etc. It is understandable that, being so fundamental as well as so familiar in relation to the various aspects of foreign policy, the spatial dimension has not attracted much attention in its general bearing upon the definition of the national interest.

In the first instance, three basic spatial aspects of the state itself must be briefly mentioned. These are its territorial character, its boundaries, and its 'vital core' or 'nerve centre'. *Territory*, along with the people and government, is indisputably an essential ingredient of the state. Indeed, there is much force in the argument that the 'territoriality' of the modern state is its major characteristic distinguishing it from its medieval predecessors. From the end of the religious wars of the seventeenth century until the ideological wars of this century, all major struggles were primarily over territory. Although serious doubts exist over the existence of a 'territorial imperative'[3] of general validity, it is clear that people fight much more determinedly in defence of their territory and that its security forms the central core of all conceptions of national interest.

The territory of a state is delimited by fixed *boundaries* which are of paramount importance since, in legal theory, within them the state enjoys complete sovereign authority and no other state is entitled to trespass across them. In real life the situation does not fully correspond with this theory. With the advance of modern technology, state boundaries have lost much of their importance. No state is any longer impenetrable; all are increasingly vulnerable to strategic, economic and psychological penetration and complete state sovereignty over a territory is gradually receding into the realm of legal fiction. The 'crisis of the territorial state' has now gone so far that we may have reached a situation resembling that at the end of the Middle

Ages when 'the gunpowder revolution' had rendered vulnerable and untenable the existing small political units, hitherto relatively secure behind their walls and moats.[4] Undoubtedly, it would be rash to forecast the demise of the territorial state within the foreseeable future, but it is clear that cross-national forces which weaken it are rapidly increasing in importance.

The exact extent of the '*vital core*' of any country is bound to be uncertain. It includes the 'nerve centre'—the capital housing the central government organization—the major metropolitan concentration of the population, and the major industrial complex. Usually the three overlap but are not completely congruent except in undeveloped countries; in all industrialized countries they are grouped together with extensive conurbations. Large and highly developed countries may possess more than one such vital centre. The United States has three distinct 'cores': on the eastern and the western seaboards and on the Great Lakes; in the Soviet Union such centres can be distinguished around Moscow, Leningrad, and the industrial and mining industries' complexes in the Ukraine and the Urals. Since the 'nerve centres' are vulnerable to nuclear attack, the superpowers have also prepared relatively safe underground emergency centres which could, if necessary, take over the essential control functions.

The 'vital core' plays a centre part in the spatial calculations relating to foreign policy. It obviously must be defended but it does not receive absolute priority. On the contrary, since the peripheral parts of the state are often less developed and more vulnerable, they may require a greater concentration of governmental effort. The ideas of equalizing economic and social development and standards of living, pressures from national minorities, regional discontents, and the dangers of subversion, particularly dangerous in border areas, all broaden the reference of the national interest from the capital and the 'vital core' to the whole of the country.

Distance is the fundamental idea underlying any spatial thinking. The notion of distance from the territory of the state, or, somewhat more precisely, from its 'nerve centre', is an essential although, as yet, poorly conceptualized ingredient in assessing the relevance—positive or negative—of the elements of the international environment as well as that of the capabilities possessed by the state. The idea of distance is based upon the implicit assumption that the state in question is the centre of things, as the distances are measured from its 'vital core'. In the case of major powers this self-centred starting point is often given a physical expression in the shape of maps of the world centred upon them. The globe does, indeed, look quite different according to whether it is transferred to a Soviet Union—or to a United-States-centred map; when they look at their respective maps, both the Russians and the Americans find support for their views that they are encircled and hence endangered.

De Gaulle is the statesman who has most clearly articulated in our generation the central position assumed for his own country. He had already, in 1945, gone on record that France is the only European country with outlets simultaneously into the Channel, the North Sea, the Atlantic and the Mediterranean, and hence occupies a key position in Europe. Moreover, he pointed out, one has only to look on a map to realize that France is also exactly between the two superpowers, the extreme point of the east towards the west and likewise the bridgehead of the west in the east. His political conclusion was therefore that the French should hold themselves strictly in the balance. He upheld this geographical image and acted upon the political conclusions drawn from it when he came to power in 1958.

In theory a state can take an 'azimuthal' view of its national interest and measure distance, by whatever yardsticks it chooses to do so, equally in all directions. In practice, however, such a view is untenable as no state has equal interests in all directions or sufficient resources to warrant an azimuthal strategy; all states are forced to choose some direction at the cost of neglecting others. Therefore the widespread criticism of de Gaulle's azimuthal strategy was fully justified as the doctrine was vague to the point of meaninglessness and, moreover, the military capabilities of France were and are much too weak a base even for a sounder global strategy.

Characteristically even the two superpowers are gradually retracting from what can be regarded as azimuthal strategies (although they have not been called so) based on the view that a menace from the fellow-superpower anywhere in the world is of roughly equal seriousness. Reversing the traditional importance attached to Asia by the isolationists apprehensive of involvement in Europe, under the impact of the Vietnam debacle, the Americans seem to be retracting from Asia. The Russians who had given up close interest in Asia in the late 1920s when the continent had disappointed the Comintern expectation that it would become a 'storm centre', are now increasingly preoccupied by the menace they perceive from China and are turning towards Asia. The growing *détente* between the two superpowers can thus be convincingly interpreted in spatial terms as being based upon differentiated trends in the main direction of their respective national interests which allow a fair degree of disengagement.

Physical distance is the simplest, but, as may be surmised, also the most misleading yardstick for measurement. In the words of George F. Kennan which relate to power but equally apply to interests:

> The effectiveness of the power radiated from any national centre decreases in proportion to the distance involved . . . Geopolitical theories of spheres of influence and stable balances of power between widely separated large and small countries frequently presume such proportional or linear decreases of military strength over distance. Yet the relation has never been so simple.[5]

The attraction of measuring distance in physical terms is increased by the availability of geographical maps on which distance can be easily assessed. This, however, requires some sophistication to avoid the pitfalls created by the problems of transferring distances from a three-dimensional globe to a two-dimensional sheet of paper; any projection can scale down true distances only in one direction and distortion in all other directions is inevitable. Hence the prevalent type of projection exercises a powerful influence upon our spatial image; an example being the popular Mercator projection which has had profound effects upon United States strategic thought.[6]

As thinking on the subject has become more sophisticated, measurements in miles or kilometres have come to be regarded as merely the 'banal distance',[7] much less important than distance computed in the social terms of time and cost of transport. While physical distance is constant, economically and socially defined distance changes with the evolution of communication. Thus, the crucial strategic aspects of national interest were fundamentally altered first by the evolution of fast, efficient and cheap water transport, then by the development of the railways, and lately by the development of aviation and of missiles. To take a current example, physical distance is only one, and by no means the decisive element in determining the strategic positions of the protagonists in Vietnam. Equally and perhaps even more relevant is the fact that both for the Americans and for the Chinese, short-distance lift facilities within the combat theatre fall far short of the long-distance lift facilities; moreover, it is the latter which are likely to improve in efficiency and decrease in cost in the next decade.[8]

Distance, measured both in physical and in economic and social terms, comes to bear upon national interest only through its perception by the decision makers which can thus be regarded as an intervening variable. This perception can be of crucial importance as social distance can be measured by varied yardsticks the implications of which are hard to grasp and interpret in the light of rapid technological change so that the images can grossly deviate from reality. The decision makers' sentiments, both of friendship and of hostility, strongly affect the perception of distance and contribute to what may be called 'psychological distance'. They determine the *direction* in which the major interests of the state are sought and pursued.

History abounds in examples of grave misjudgements of distance in which the decision makers' sentiments, often their wishful thinking, played a prominent part. Thus, in 1938 Neville Chamberlain thought of Czechoslovakia as a country too remote to involve sufficiently vital British national interests to contemplate going to war over them. He was disabused in the following year. In the 1930s Norway perceived herself as peripherally located and hence free to abstain from conflicts among great powers and to pursue a policy of neutrality; only when, as the result of the German invasion, the Norwegian leaders found themselves in exile, did they see Norway's position as 'exposed' or 'strategic'.[9]

It is also possible to err in the opposite direction, by failing to recognize the extent of actual distances. This is a way of interpreting the foreign policy of the Australians who, in the face of physical distance and the consequent costs of transport, had traditionally regarded themselves as being closest to Britain and, since the Second World War, to the United States. The fall of Singapore and ultimately the decision to withdraw from east of Suez have brought home the extent of Britain's distance; the current revision of the American commitments in Asia, that of the United States. Australia is clearly much closer to Asia than to either. Arguably, misjudgement of the extent of actual distances was an important factor in the strategic over-commitment of Britain and of the United States since 1945.

The following general hypotheses can be advanced about the role of the spatial dimension of the national interest:

1   Physical distance is an important but by no means decisive variable; it does not necessarily prevail

against historical, ethnic, cultural, sentimental and other interests.

2   Changes in the technology of transport greatly affect the impact of physical distance. The transition has been dramatic in the case of Antarctica, a region which, until recently, could scarcely be reached but which may soon become available for commercial exploitation of minerals and for strategic uses.

3   Distance measured by economic and social yard-sticks, is affected by the capabilities of the individual state. Thus the distance from South-East Asia is much greater for, say, Costa Rica than for the United States. Britain, with her contracting strategic capa-bilities, and Japan, with her expanding ones, are reinterpreting the spatial dimensions of their respec-tive national interests in opposite directions, Britain withdrawing from east of Suez, and Japan gradually though slowly expanding the territorial range of her interests.

4   The distance of an interest from the 'vital core' of the state is a convenient starting point, but it requires modification in each individual case, following con-siderations under 1.

5   The amount of modification necessary correlates with the power status. The higher this is, the more likely is a state to add interests in nodal strategic and communication points which are spatially remote, whereas smaller Powers tend to have only economic interests outside the immediately adjoining regions.

6   The spatial dimension is less significant for the two superpowers than for other states for two additional reasons. First, as long as they attribute central im-portance to their mutual competition, their interests

anywhere, however distant from their respective 'vital cores', must be regarded as vital; this outlook, as has been argued, may now be passing. Second, both possess the capabilities to reduce the impact of physical distance to the technologically possible limits. In some significant respects the strategic distance between the United States and the Soviet Union is less than that between such contiguous countries as Libya and Tunisia or Bolivia and Paraguay. The dramatic shortening of this distance is shown by the strategies of nuclear deterrence and also by the location of the two major post-war outbreaks of violence in Korea and Vietnam, countries remote from both superpowers.[10]

7   Distance is a crucial variable in the intensity of interaction between any states but it does not determine either bad or good relations; history provides no conclusive evidence that either the 'good neighbour' or the 'bad neighbour' (*mandala*) theory is correct.

8   It should be within the scope of cartography, which is a highly evolved art, to provide useful graphic presentations of the spatial dimension of the national interest for purposes of comparison, using not only physical but also economic, social and strategic distances. Superimposing the map of one state over that of another would reveal, at a glance, the significant similarities and discrepancies in the spatial dimension of any aspects of their respective national interests in which distance plays a significant part.

Regionalism is an aspect of foreign policy in which the spatial dimension is prominent. It is sometimes discussed as the influence of the geographical factors which the state cannot fully escape ('regional pulls' or even 'the regional imperative') and sometimes as a matter of deliberate choice. Thus, in the arguments of the pro-Europeans, Britain cannot escape the facts of her position as an island off the shores of Western Europe, whereas her membership of the Atlantic region or of the Commonwealth, if we choose to call it a region, is a voluntary act of policy.[11]

Most geographers today agree that it is futile to try to define geographical regions in general terms and they endeavour to do so only for specific purposes which allow them to use appropriate criteria. It is equally futile to try to define a political region in general terms. The essence of such a region seems to be that international relations within it are integrated to a greater extent than they are within global politics as a whole. In the terminology of systems analysis, a region is a sub-system within the international system; its boundaries are constituted by discontinuities in the political interaction relevant for the region. This, however, does not mean that a single member may not maintain relations more intensive and more relevant to the region with some outsider than with some other members of the region. Thus, United States or United Arab Republic relations with the Soviet Union are, by many criteria, more intensive and more significant for the regional affairs of the Western Hemisphere and of the Middle East respectively than their relations with many, possibly the majority, of the states within the regions themselves.

The physical and social features which constitute a geographical region do not in themselves constitute also a political one as, for this purpose, they must be accompanied by a politically significant interaction of sufficient intensity. Empirical indices can be sought for such interaction, e.g. diplomatic and military co-operation is expressed in the size of trade and aid. It is, however, much harder to find indices for the bonds of ideology, whether they are positive, as Communism in Eastern Europe, or negative, as anti-Communism in the Western Hemisphere. For countries such as Israel or Cuba, which are located in regions hostile to them, interaction can be measured, although not very persuasively, by indices of hostile behaviour. Sometimes the boundaries of a political region are fairly clearly defined as those of Scandinavia, but sometimes they are uncertain and disputed as those of the Middle East.

By definition, a region has a political structure peculiar to it and separate from global politics. This may take the form of a sphere of influence of a leading power which can assume many forms as manifested by the histories of the Western Hemisphere and of Eastern Europe. It may include a state to which the other members are hostile—such as Israel or Cuba—but which plays a significant, though negative role in regional politics. The region may be subdivided, as Europe now is into East and West and, within the latter, into the Six and EFTA; it may include several states of the same rank, as did the Concert of Europe in the nineteenth century.

Within a regional context, the definition of the national interest is governed by considerations similar to those within the global context. What is unique, and of fundamental importance, is the decision as to which regional context is most relevant.

Small states situated within an organized region have little choice but to accommodate themselves to being a member of it and to define their national interest in regional terms (Czechoslovakia or Rumania in Eastern Europe, the small Central American republics in the Western Hemisphere). They have more freedom of manoeuvre when they are on the periphery of the region from which position they can seek outside assistance (Israel, Cuba), or use this possibility to assert a degree of autonomy or neutrality (Yugoslavia, Austria). A group of small states situated on the periphery of a region can contemplate the establishment of a sub-region as an alternative or as a method of ensuring a greater degree of autonomy within it (Scandinavia, and the various African groupings). Even small states occasionally face fundamental choices in which the several relevant regional spheres can be conceptualized. Thus, during the Second

World War, the fundamental basis for wartime political thinking by the Norwegian leaders in exile was provided by looking
at Norway's post-war role in terms of being, in order of priority,
a United Nations state, a maritime state, an Atlantic state, a
North Sea state, and a Scandinavian state.[12]

Such choices more frequently confront great powers which are
or can become regional leaders. Immediately after the war, the
United States played this role in the North Atlantic basin,
whereas Britain neglected her potential leadership role in
Western Europe; Sweden was unsuccessful in her indecisive
initiative to organize a Scandinavian Security Pact as a substitute for participation in NATO because she insisted upon retaining full neutrality.[13]

Greater powers frequently belong to more than one region
but only the two superpowers can be considered today as world
powers in a sense that their interests are worldwide and that
they do not, therefore, opt out of any regional alignments although, naturally, they accord them different priorities. Greater
powers with smaller capabilities are faced with a decision as to
which region to choose as the major sphere of their international
activities. Thus, although British participation in the Western
European region which is no longer blocked by President de
Gaulle is now the avowed governmental policy and can be supported by powerful arguments, it cannot be regarded as inevitable. In fact, throughout the post-war period, the major
argument about British foreign policy was based upon the
recognition that Britain belongs to three distinct spheres:
Western Europe, the Atlantic community and the Commonwealth. The political choice which prevailed was to give priority
to what was called the 'special relationship' with the United
States, with the Commonwealth coming next, and Europe third.
By the 1960s, all hope of organizing the Commonwealth into
something approaching a political region had completely failed;
Britain became increasingly disillusioned about the possibilities
of continuing and cultivating her 'special relationship' with the

United States, and hence she turned to Europe. Since, for a long time, her entry was effectively blocked, participation in Western Europe remained only a possibility and still has to compete with the proposals for the alternative of a North Atlantic Free Trade Association. Also the Commonwealth ties may be ultimately preserved and even strengthened as the result of a re-evaluation following the decision to withdraw from east of Suez.

A similar choice confronted President Nasser who, in his early book,[14] analysed Egypt's position within three spheres: the Arab world, Africa and the Moslem world. He decided to accord them priority in this order. Despite periodical setbacks, Egypt has played a leading role among the Arabs and her main stress has been upon the Middle Eastern region. Within the African region, Nasser's ambitions for leadership have been disappointed but he carefully maintains his membership which enables him to obstruct the growing links between some African states and Israel, and to secure him diplomatic support in the United Nations. The political organization of the Moslem world into something approaching a region is distinctly less promising than the other two alignments, and Nasser has not tried it out.

Finally, to cite another politically important example, Germany, straddling across the Great European Plain and being a bridge between Western and Eastern Europe, has traditionally oscillated between the two. In the post-war period Dr. Adenauer determinedly steered the Federal Republic of Germany into a firm Western alignment. Now, however, both the chancellor and his policy are dead and the Germans have not attained the reunification which they had been vaguely promised would follow from a 'position of strength'. As any form of unification clearly depends upon Soviet goodwill, the Germans are bound to consider the diverse variants of the two logical alternatives to their present policy, namely a form of neutrality between East and West and a form of rapprochement with the East for which they can find historical precedents in the Rapallo tradition.

The time dimension

Time, as much as space, is such a fundamental category of thinking that it defies clear conceptualization; no human actions or thoughts can be conceived outside its context and yet they rarely have fixed points of reference to it. This is due to the nature of the flow of time which is continuous; within it, the present is merely the point at which the past and the future overlap. Not the whole of human existence is affected by this flow in an identical manner. One of the most striking phenomena in social life is 'the contemporaneity of the non-contemporaneous', the coexistence at any given point of time of phenomena related to various points of the past and of the future. In times of rapid change the mixture is incongruous, as in our generation when, as has been so often observed, our 'horse and buggy' modes of thinking and institutions cannot cope with the problems arising from the technology of the nuclear age.

Foreign policy is no exception. National interest is involved whether we are dealing with current problems, or with plans for the future, or with the evaluation of the past. It is rarely, if ever, possible to relate any of its issues or formulations to one of the three tenses in an exclusive fashion; we can, however, try to arrange them in a spectrum based upon their relationship to time. They will fall somewhere between one extreme of formulations firmly rooted in the past and another one of those deliberately looking forward to the future; in political argument these extremes are often called respectively, outdated and utopian. (Professor Morgenthau has proposed a distinction between three levels of international theory[15] which roughly corresponds with the three tenses: the level of history which deals with the past; the level of attempts at reform concerned mainly with the present; and the level of pragmatic manipulation which is related to the future.)

There is little hope that we shall ever achieve a *general* agreement about the ranking of interests in their relation to time but there are fair prospects of partial success, provided we limit the exercise to a specific aspect or issue of the national interest. There is less hope for the successful ordering of all the aspects. National interest is such a congeries of 'non-contemporaneous' elements that it is hard to conceive empirical indicators for a systematic arrangement of these elements in terms of their relevance for the concept as well as in terms of their reference to time.

Another quality of interests which is related to time is their duration, the two extremes here being permanent and ephemeral interests. The major determinant of location within this spectrum is the level of generality at which the national interest is perceived. When we think in terms of national self-perpetuation national interest is as permanent as the modern state system and is coeval with the national state involved. When we think of 'sovereignty' as the legal expression of this self-perpetuation and of defence as its major foundation, we find that they go equally far back in the past but increasing numbers of thinkers claim that they are not likely to persist for very long in the future—meaning that they are not quite so permanent. The permanent quality of the more specific so-called 'permanent interests' is doubtful not only in respect to the future, but also regarding their past.[16]

At the other extreme, short-range, tactical aspects of foreign policy invariably include interests so ephemeral that nobody, or very few would include them in the notion of the national interest at all, except in the heat of the contemporary political argument. Thus the interest of the United States in supporting anti-Communist leaders and the Soviet interest in supporting leaders sympathetic to Communism, inevitably leads to constant reversals of tactics in countries where leadership frequently changes.

The propensity to orientate the national interest either towards the past or towards the future may conceivably be correlated with some identifiable characteristics of the state or of the 'national character' or style. It is a subject well worth investigating. The major feature of the international systems until now has been the clash between the individual national interests of the member states. If adequate methods are to be devised for reducing this central conflict, their success will largely depend upon these states reformulating their respective national interests in a less antagonistic manner; hence qualities conducive to orientation to the future will need to be cultivated.

Here a major variable may be found in the anticipated changes in the net achievement capability. The more a state is convinced that this capability is likely to diminish and hence that its interests are less likely to be secured, the greater the incentive for it to reformulate and reduce these interests. Conversely, the greater the confidence that the state's net achievement capability is likely to be maintained or improved, the greater the likelihood of retaining existing formulations or increasing the demands. There is an obvious correlation between conservative views and attachment to tradition and an orientation towards the past, and, conversely, between radical or revolutionary views and ideology and an orientation towards the future. Nevertheless, owing to the dialectical nature of political argument, there is no complete overlap. In all ages there exist contradictory streams of political thought which, with the passage of time, may, but need not necessarily, alter their character. Thus, in the course of time, a revolutionary tradition may remain truly revolutionary as well as become rather conservative; conversely, a conservative tradition often includes elements which, within a future context, may become quite radical. The conservative-radical spectrum is, therefore, relevant only in general terms, as an expression of a rather vague tendency.

The formulation of the national interest is not a matter of a continuous assessment, each phase of which can be dated. The salience of its various elements constantly changes but reformulation takes place only sporadically, when a major decision has to be made. With time, the formulation inevitably dates and, although it may remain in force in its original form for a long time, it is likely to be increasingly deviated from until the discrepancy becomes flagrant or a new assessment is called for by some sudden change. Only then is national interest reformulated. The relationship between these continuous slight changes and explicit reformulations can be best explained by likening it to the play of colours in a kaleidoscope. The kaleidoscope is repeatedly gently shaken in order to pick out the varying colours in the light, but occasionally is shaken more violently so that an entirely new pattern emerges. It may not always be fully clear whether the rearrangement is due more to a violent shake-up or to an accumulation of slight changes.

Even this rather complicated comparison is far too simple to convey reality. First, the dating of the formulation of an interest is by no means easy. Each decision is the culminating point of a chain of decision making which is often long and complex; it is the essence of sophisticated historical research to trace its origins increasingly further back. Second, we cannot assume that there is a hierarchical relation between the final formulation and the subsequent decisions and actions; in fact, without any explicit reformulation, fundamental changes in definition can arise by implication, both in action and in argument.

However indecisive all our reasoning may be, we can get some intimation of the chronological order in which the various issues had been formulated and determined, provided political argument provides us at least with occasional evidence. This, however, is the case only in liberal democratic countries and only on those issues on which our political institutions and mass media do not fail us. Where such argument cannot be openly conducted, either owing to repressive censorship or to an ignorant and indifferent public opinion, or to a combination of the two, evidence for proceeding with such time-ordering is even more limited. Nevertheless, it may be worth while speculating on the possibility that to some, perhaps definable extent, the dichotomies and incongruities of foreign policy may be attributable to the fact that the various aspects of the national interest are determined in different periods of time. Some major questions should be investigated. Does explicit formulation increase the tendency for these discrepancies, since fully articulated policy tends to become less flexible? Conversely, does a stable formulation based upon a firm ideological basis ensure greater uniformity or does it actually increase the confusion by preventing reformulation even when this confusion has become intense? How does the relatively short history affect the formulation of the national interest in the new states?

The difference in the time dimension between the operational and the aspirational levels of definition of the national interest does not lie in their reference to the past or the future; each is concerned with both. The major discrepancy lies in the time-span taken into account. At the operational level it tends to be shorter; at the aspirational level decision makers are less concerned with the contingencies of the present and hence look both further back into the past and further forward into the future.

At the explanatory and polemical level, both the past and the future serve as sources of arguments and of rationalizations. A person selecting them is bound to be guided by the convenience of the occasion and by the character and often the average age of the public addressed.

National successes in the past encourage reference to them and so do national prospects for success in the future. It may prove possible to specify with some degree of precision the relationship of political arguments to the time scale by applying content analysis to statements made on different occasions in the course of a national debate of single issues as well as by comparing debates on different issues and by engaging in cross-national comparisons.

Part II
The Formulation of National Interest

6/The Structure of Decision Making

The process
No two individual estimates of how national interests are formulated are likely to be identical as they depend upon the position one chooses on a whole number of issues, the major ones of which are discussed in the following chapter. All comprehensive accounts must, however, include three distinct elements which can be regarded as independent and simultaneously interconnected variables: the decision makers and their international and domestic environments. A behaviourally oriented analysis must also include the concept of 'the image' held by the decision makers of their environment which is an intervening variable between them.

The analysis of decision making in foreign policy[1] can be adapted to the study of the ways in which national interest is determined; in fact the latter merely refers to decision making in the area of the values pursued in foreign policy. One important difference must be noted: whereas, despite its complexities, foreign policy as a whole is a form of political behaviour which yields to behavioural analysis, it is in the nature of the vague and nebulous concept of 'national interest' that the process by which it is arrived at is much more diffuse and unclear. It is, nevertheless, an essentially political process in which political argument, with its appeals to reason, as well as emotions play a dominant role. It is possible, though difficult, to subject it to a rational analysis.

In the West we tend to accept the Aristotelian model of politics, the essence of which is the competition between power groups associated with the diverse and competing interests, values and goals as well as the varying means for their attainment. The final choices depend more upon the relative power of these groups than upon the cogency of the arguments.[2] Although the institutional forms in Communist countries and in new states are very different from ours, it is possible to apply to them the same model, although both the power struggle and the argumentation take different forms.

The rationality of political argument is generally spurious as its aim is to convince the public to which it is directed and not to achieve logical clarification. The alleged 'reasons' are often no more than plausible rationalizations. The spurious character of the arguments dealing with the national interest is usually even more pronounced for the simple reason that the only logical measurement of rationality can be found in an end-means relationship, in seeking the most appropriate ways to achieve postulated objectives. There are no such rational yardsticks for the selection of priorities among values which are the main area of decisions about national interest. As this is an important characteristic of the arguments about the national interest, after the discussion of the agencies concerned with the process of choice, their images, motivations and values in this chapter, the following chapter includes sections on the clarity and rationality of the end-product of the process. No attempt is made to analyse the domestic and international environment within which the decision makers operate in real life as their influence upon the formulation of national interest is only indirect, through the medium of the images held by them.

To use Parsonian terminology, being in charge of a national system, a government must be concerned with four fundamental functions: systems maintenance, adaptation to the natural and human environments, goal attainment and integration. Two further specific functions of basic importance should be added: goal setting and self-transformation.[3] It is unnecessary to go into the intricacies of the full meaning of these categories in order to realize that each of the functions distinguished involves some elements of foreign policy and also that they endeavour to categorize what any definition of the national interest must include.

The formulation of the national interest which is the subject of this chapter falls squarely under the function of the setting of goals. We can conceive of this formulation, as of all processes of choice, as an interplay between the decision makers and the relevant environment in which they endeavour to pursue their values and to attain their objectives by finding suitable means and by dealing with the restraints and obstacles encountered. Employing the distinction outlined in Chapter 2, when national interests are conceived of as aspirations, the value element in this interplay is stressed, whereas operationally conceived interests result in greater relevance being attached to the environment. The basic scheme of decision making is fundamentally identical: all chains of decisions must start with an assessment of both the value component—whether it consists mainly of aspirations or of concrete goals—and of the environmental circumstances in as much detail as is deemed relevant for the former. The two are confronted and a decision is reached on the basis of a calculation of the probabilities of success and of cost; it is followed by implementing decisions and by evaluations. This is merely an analytical schematization. In real life the processes are, of course, infinitely more complex. The interplay between the decision makers and their environment is continuous and allows for countless permutations; the specific sequences, stages and phases do not follow each other in logical order but frequently get blurred; conscious rational decisions appear to be the exception rather than the rule. Nevertheless, schematization and simplification are the only ways in which we can impose the logical order necessary for comprehending the chaos of real life.

The agencies

Not all the agencies and processes involved in the making of foreign policy can be expected to be equally relevant for the expression of national interest. If, as has been done here, the notion of 'national interest' is taken to be more or less co-terminous with that of the purpose of foreign policy and if full account is taken of the fact that this purpose is rarely, if ever, fully articulated, obviously only the highest central organs should be normally concerned with it. In fact, this is, generally speaking, true. The nation's aspirations are obviously determined by the very top decision makers. They are also the only people capable of thinking about the whole aggregate of national interest at the operational level and they are the only people with the authority to make appropriate official declarations and statements. At the same time, at the operational level, the actual detailed conduct of foreign policy requires at least an occasional consideration of its purpose and this is done by the officials actually dealing with any issue. Thus the perennial tension between centralization and decentralization recurs here in the form of tension between the central responsibility for the formulation of the aspirations and of operational policies in general terms as well as for explanation, and the responsibility at lower levels for the operational detail.

Allowing for the close but incomplete correlation between the making of foreign policy and the formulation of national interest, the hypothesis can be advanced that two major variables affect the degree of centralization: first, the power status of the state and, second, the nature of the regime and the level of popular participation.

In small states, the scope of national interest is narrower than in great powers and so are the extent of governmental machinery and the range of the problems facing them; moreover, one of these problems is often salient or even overwhelming, as it affects their very survival. Therefore national interest can be formulated and a coherent policy can be prescribed at the very top without much difficulty. In greater powers, the scope of the national interest is broader, the governmental machinery more complex, and the range of problems much greater. It is difficult or even impossible for the top decision makers to cope with the masses of uneven and unco-ordinated information and to comprehend the cross-currents of conflicting forces; they cannot help concentrating on what is salient at the time, hence attempts made at the top at achieving a coherent foreign policy are unlikely to be fully successful and a degree of decentralization persists. Britain with her well evolved diplomatic service is a classical example.[5]

We may plausibly assume that under a democratic regime with broad popular participation, national discussions frequently take place and elements other than the central government participate in the formulation of national interest; conversely, that an autocratic regime and poor political participation result in centralization. Hence it can be expected that in Communist states, where governments are autocratic or in new states where political participation is limited, the process of formulation is more centralized than in western democracies.

All the agencies involved in the political process and, specifically, in the making of foreign policy, can be relevant in the formulation of national interest. They are considered here only from that angle;[6] discussion is inevitably restricted mainly to western democracies since elsewhere the process is highly centralized.

One of the decisive variables in determining the nature of a political system is the role of the opposition.[7] Opposition, is, of course, possible only in a reasonably sophisticated as well as democratic political system based upon a fundamental consensus that it should be continued without fundamental changes, where non-governmental groups and public opinion at large are both sufficiently informed and sufficiently free to take a stand on foreign policy. An institutionalized opposition is unthinkable in states insufficiently integrated or those under unpopular regimes, or when the political culture is very low. Hence the attempts at introducing a Westminster model of democracy in African states invariably failed whereas the Communist regimes have been ruthlessly suppressing the possibility of organized, articulate opposition, as exemplified by the 1968 intervention in Czechoslovakia. Needless to say, the elimination of political opposition by these systems does not eliminate dissent and discontent, and these find their channels of expression although they cannot be easily articulated.

In fact, even in the pluralist democratic systems, the ideal of an opposition the business of which is to oppose, to keep a clear view of alternatives and to propose new options regarding national interests, to take defined stands based upon principle and to question the working of the institutions and the very foundations of the system, is not really representative of political reality. In recent decades, the technique of the open debate, of the argument which should prevail and secure the support of the majority of the electorate, has, to a large extent, given way to the technique of consensus in which controversial issues are reduced to the lowest common denominator acceptable to all. Even in the heyday of western democratic institutions in the nineteenth century, the effectiveness of opposition was, on the whole, limited to domestic issues. In the twentieth century, consensus on foreign policy which was imperative during the two prolonged world wars has been elevated to the pedestal of a principle of national unity to be achieved also in peace time. Governments appeal to the electors and opposition parties to take important issues of foreign policy out of the heat of party strife. The phenomenon is universal. The United States has evolved the ideal of 'bipartisanship'; in Britain the near unanimity in 1969 on major foreign policy issues between Prime Minister Wilson and Edward Heath, the leader of the opposition, was matched in the past, especially during the period of 'butskellism'; in Western Germany the Social Democrats lost most of their independence when they joined the 'Great Coalition'; in the Fifth Republic throughout de Gaulle's rule there was no effective opposition at all. Whichever the actual system, there is apparently a strong general tendency for the foreign policy stands of the opposition and the government to converge.

Continuity in the interpretation of important national interests has, of course, the advantage of showing a unity of national purpose and of ensuring that a change in the identity of the ruling party does not involve a fundamental change in foreign policy. When Mr. Wilson became seriously perturbed about the credibility of Britain's resolve to join Europe, to dispel the doubts entertained in de Gaulle's France, he appointed Mr. Soames, both a staunch pro-European and prominent Conservative, as the British ambassador to Paris. When presenting his credentials to the French president, the new ambassador stressed that this appointment by the Labour government of a member of its Conservative predecessor 'is a sign of the national nature of our policies towards France in particular and Europe in general'.[8]

The opposition is poorly equipped to challenge governmental definitions of the national interest for several reasons. First, it lacks independent sources of information equal to those commanded by the government; Churchill seems to be the last individual statesman who managed, in the 1930s, to build up a satisfactory independent information network. Only in the United States the standing committees of the Senate and of the House of Representatives command reasonable information sources of their own. Indeed, the United States is the only country in which effective opposition to the current governmental definition of national interest occasionally arises, on the lines of the competition between the legislature and executive. The major opponent of President Johnson's foreign policy was not the leader of the Republican party but Senator Fulbright, the Democratic chairman of the Foreign Relations Committee of the Senate.

Second, serious opposition which aspires to rule must try to appear capable of forming a responsible government and must appeal to the majority of the electorate. In order to secure the support of the middle-of-the-road majority it tends to eschew fundamental, controversial and extreme problems and formulations, which may affect the principle of national unity. Lacking not only a 'counter-bureaucracy' but also a 'counter-ideology', opposition generally fails in the important role it is theoretically capable of performing—providing an instrumentality for constant rethinking, for innovation, for considering alternatives and for weighing options. All it can achieve is to prod the government to be somewhat more articulate in its definitions and to amend them marginally rather than fundamentally. It is characteristic that discussion of the basic choices on vital interests cannot be readily accommodated within the framework of party competition. This is equally true about Britain's attitudes to Europe, about the United States' involvement in Vietnam, and about German unification problems. Radical opposition does not appeal to the electorate[9] and also tends to become disloyal which may lead to its suppression by the government in power. Although we tend to believe that democratic systems have certain built-in restraints upon powerful individual decision makers which curb them from arriving at potentially disastrous decisions, the possibility of a public debate and of an effective opposition ultimately arising are not a full guarantee against ill-considered and ill-conceived decisions. To take three somewhat comparable examples, in this respect there is a certain amount of similarity between the British Suez expedition in 1956, the United States' involvement in Vietnam since 1964 and the Soviet intervention in Czechoslovakia in 1968. All that may be surmised is that a possibility of public debate at least reduces the probability of such decisions being taken.

The interaction between the government in the narrow sense of the word (the executive) and the other governmental organs as well as social groupings, greatly varies from country to country and also from period to period. The variety is greatest in the United States, both owing to its federal structure and to the broad scope of its interests. Only in the United States does the legislature play a really important role in the formulation of foreign policy. In opposing centralized presidential powers, the Congress '. . . rested its case for equal power on the fact that it represents not some merely generalized national interest, such as the President purports to represent all the time, but rather the whole living nation in all its multiplicity and variety.'[10]

It is also in the United States that owing to the size and complexity of bureaucracy some of its branches have the greatest chance of asserting themselves in the formulation of national interests. The most pronounced has been the role of the Central Intelligence Agency which, it is generally argued, over a period of years has been conducting a foreign policy of its own based upon its idiosyncratic definition of national interest as consisting predominantly of opposition to Communism.

A general hypothesis can be advanced with a fair degree of confidence that the influence of bureaucracy is roughly proportional to the scope and intricacy of governmental business: the larger the organization the lesser the chance of the people at the top of acquainting themselves personally with all the details even of the most salient issues. They are perforce informed by, and to a large extent governed by, the advice tendered to them by civil servants and by military advisers. These officials, however, are fundamentally ill-equipped to consider the purpose of foreign policy which lies in achieving certain objectives within the international environment. Their immediate objective is to satisfy the president or the prime minister by presenting him with acceptable information and by implementing the political objectives determined by him. According to the requirements of the political system, they may also have to satisfy the parliament, public opinion and/or the relevant major interest groups.

In the United States where presidential powers as well as the inadequacies of the bureaucratic system are great, personal political advisers to the President, whose role has now become institutionalized, have been prominent. Colonel House, Harry Hopkins, Professor Kissinger, undoubtedly all played central roles in the definition of United States national interests during their periods of influence. The pattern of absorbing the expertise of natural scientists through institutionalizing their role in determining national defence problems has not yet been fully repeated in the field of social sciences through institutionalizing a broader association of independent academic experts on foreign policy,[11] although consultation and 'farming out' of research projects are widespread. Other states have not followed the American pattern although the divorce between governmental activities and academic research is no longer as great as in the past.

In the absence of reliable detailed information it is hard to ascertain the real role of bureaucracies in Communist great powers, as, for example, the extent to which criticisms of the bureaucratization of the Soviet Union under Stalin are justified. How much of the actual power wrenched from the party did Stalin vest in his shadowy 'technical cabinet'?[12] Whether the Communist system happens to labour under 'the cult of personality' or endeavours to free itself from it, its leaders seem to intervene much more frequently than in the West and seem to pursue their aspirations with much less attention to operational problems and the costs and risk involved. In small states, the leaders can make decisions more easily and often without or even against bureaucratic advice; there are fewer advisers and more scope for the significant element of personal insight which, with greater powers, is considered as some kind of aberration, as in the case of British Prime Minister Eden in the Suez crisis.

This practice is usual in new states, but occurs also in the West. Thus, the crucial negotiations with the Russians in April 1938 were handled by the Finnish prime minister and foreign minister alone, who, moreover, rejected the advice of their chief military adviser, Marshal Mannerheim.[13] The equally crucial decision to exclude Singapore from the Malaysian Federation in 1965 was taken personally by the Malaysian prime minister in the isolation of a London clinic where he was divorced from the direct advice of his political associates and officials. He followed his custom of relying upon his intuition based upon his unique political experience.[14]

The personality of the head of the government is an important variable in all states, not only those which are small or weakly organized. Some individuals are organization men, ready to listen to and to follow advice, others are individualists. Even within the well-established British traditions, occasionally prime ministers decide issues of paramount importance outside the normal constitutional procedures, as Chamberlain handled appeasement or Eden the Suez crisis. In the United States, Franklin Roosevelt, Truman or Kennedy with their determination to make personal decisions may be contrasted with Eisenhower.

Pressure groups in the western sense exist only in western democratic systems, but their equivalents, similarly active in the definition of national interests, can be found also in all other states, even when these are fairly autocratic. For instance the Catholic church in Poland openly declared itself in favour of a rapprochement with Western Germany, thus becoming an agency advocating the loosening of complete political dependence upon the Soviet Union.

Three points should be made about the operation of such pressure groups. First, they refer to particular interests rather than to the whole, but, as soon as their claims begin to affect the national interest as a whole, the debate naturally shifts into the main channels of the political debate which, in the West, means party politics. Second, before a particular interest advanced by a pressure group becomes part and parcel of the national interest, it must be accepted as such by the appropriate official agencies.

Third, a potential clash exists between any particular interest and the national interest as a whole but the historical record of their relationship is ambiguous. It does not fully justify the

Marxist allegation that large-scale financial and industrial concerns determine the foreign policies of the capitalist countries; in fact, these concerns are often manipulated by the governments for foreign policy purposes.[15] Undoubtedly, the large concerns are influential but their self-regarding interests and ends have to be incorporated by the government in the general notion of national interest. Sometimes, perhaps quite often, selfish interests are sufficiently powerful to twist the formulation of the national interest in their favour, to the detriment of the remainder of the community. This does not, however, invariably happen as 'countervailing interests' operate within society and the government does, at least to some extent, watch the 'general good'. Moreover, it is impossible to deny a limited degree of general truth in what an American secretary of defense Charles E. Wilson rather innocently asserted that not only what is good for the United States is good also for General Motors, that the particular interest does, to some extent at least, coincide with the general good.

The role of public opinion varies with the nature of the regime and with the degree of political participation. By and large, its role in the formulation of national interest is identical with that in the formulation of foreign policy in general: in all regimes it prescribes the parameters within which this definition is politically acceptable. Obviously these parameters are much broader where public opinion has no powers of expressing itself in free elections by overthrowing the government, but leaders are never fully free from the constraints of public opinion despite the absence of opportunities for its expression and aggregation: dissent can centre around churches, armed forces, universities, popular personalities and even the most unpolitically sounding cultural and social organizations. Public opinion is, of course, frequently ignored, but not without peril.

The way in which an interest is formulated is influenced by the specific position of the decision maker who is ultimately responsible for it. One may surmise that the lower his level, the narrower the context and the fewer the elements taken into account. Consequently expertise in a given function (e.g. at the Board of Trade or the Ministry of Defence) or in a given area in a political section within the Foreign Ministry, creates a bias in favour of the speciality of the body. If the formulation is very narrow, unless the matter is relatively unimportant, there is a fair chance that the limitations of appraisal will be discovered and corrected higher up in the hierarchy. This bureaucratic safeguard is not, however, fully satisfactory as very minor decisions may unexpectedly have major repercussions. Ideally they should all be taken with the fullest possible consideration of the national interest constantly in mind.

7/Images, Motivations and Values

Images

The notion of 'the will of the people' or of 'the nation' is not meaningless but is too nebulous for the purposes of behavioural analysis. It is more rewarding to concentrate upon the actual decision makers who act on behalf of the people or nation and to regard the latter as an element of their domestic environment from which they obtain support and receive demands, which prescribes the parameters between which national interest can be determined. The nature and the numbers of the decision makers greatly vary from system to system but we can generalize about them as individuals all engaged in the same specific social roles.

As the decision-making process consists of an interaction between those making the decisions and their environment, the important intervening variable is the image[1] of this environment which they hold. The decision makers cannot take in the whole of their environment and be omniscient; their perception works selectively, choosing only a small proportion of the overwhelmingly large number of messages coming to them. The images they form are crucial for their decisions as they make these decisions on the basis of the interpretation of their perceived, psychological environment and not of real life in which their decisions have to be implemented. Needless to say, discrepancies between the psychological and the operational environments can have grave consequences, as witness the case of President Roosevelt being unaware of the Japanese task force steaming towards Pearl Harbour during the last few days of the United States and Japanese negotiations before the war. We can usefully interpret the nervous tension underlying the strategies of nuclear deterrence as a justified apprehension that the rival superpower may succeed in a technological breakthrough. This could suddenly change the operational environment so that one's strategies conceived within a psychological environment based on a now misleading image would become totally inadequate.

It is clearly essential for the decision makers to have an image of reality which does not deviate from it in any substantial respect, and therefore all states expend considerable resources on intelligence which is the only way to estimate the ecological pressures. Unfortunately, images have an affective as well as a cognitive component. Since the information perceived cannot encompass the whole of reality, all its items must pass through a filter which selects those which are deemed relevant, i.e. fit into the pattern of the image. As the *Gestalt* school of psychology has convincingly argued, a pattern, once accepted, creates blind spots for all evidence which does not fit into it. We are unreceptive to evidence which does not support our image and we tend to perpetuate the existing image, often until it catastrophically diverges from real life. We wake up to our follies when it is too late—when we have suddenly realized that disaster is impending or directly confronting us.

All sound intelligence services should therefore be separate from the executive branch and be reasonably independent in order to limit the danger of wishful thinking, that is of reading into reality what is dictated by values. The blunders of Soviet foreign policy are often quoted as a striking example of the heavy price a state has to pay for the intelligence services reporting what they think the powers-that-be wish to hear. In the West, intelligence is less faulty but falls far short of the ideal. The United States is the only country in which the division between executive and intelligence tasks is really blurred as the CIA occasionally undertakes compromising independent foreign policy activities. In all states, however, the intelligence officers are not divorced from the national value system but operate within it. Their separation from the executive tasks makes them more likely to perceive governmental blunders but does not free them from the blinding general national prejudices and biases.

The information component in policy choices is obviously of great significance but one must not exaggerate its impact. In order to save time and resources, decision makers are usually satisfied with information less complete than would be ideally desirable; through the affective components of the image into which information is fitted, it is also inevitably biased. Moreover, decisions are based not only on information but also upon values and goals; when they are reached on the basis of incomplete or misleading information it is still often doubtful whether fuller and less biased information would necessarily lead to a different decision. For instance, when the British government decided upon economic sanctions against the rebellious government of Southern Rhodesia, it was acting on the basis of an overestimate of the efficiency of such sanctions.[2] As the compelling political reason for adopting these sanctions was to prevent the application of force, it seems unlikely that a more correct anticipation of the ineffectiveness of the economic sanctions and of the spirit of resistance of the Southern Rhodesian people would have altered the nature of the decision. In all political systems, wishful thinking sometimes overrides full information if the latter indicates an unwanted course of action. Thus Stalin refused to heed the warnings about Hitler's impending attack upon Russia; de Gaulle ignored information about the extent of anti-Gaullist feelings in Dakar when he attempted a Free French landing there; Eden ignored Dulles's warning that the United States would not condone the use of force over Suez.

Sometimes the effect of information is hard to assess. For instance, during the last war for one crucial year Britain at least publicly acted as if the danger of Hitler's invasion were still imminent despite reliable intelligence that it was not. Some twenty people were privy to the information—did they entertain some doubts about its reliability or did they desire to ensure the continuation of American aid and to keep up domestic morale,[3] or, perhaps, could they simply not decide what to do? If the rulers of an underdeveloped country national-ize foreign enterprises despite clear economic intelligence that this is likely to affect adversely the country's economy, to what degree do they fail to understand the messages or disbelieve their contents, or accord priority to the political goals of eco-nomic independence, or yield to domestic pressures?

Motivations

The value component of decisions is probably much more significant than information but it is also much more complex. Despite the insatiable curiosity of the historians who probe into the motives of the actors, there is little that we can generalize about them with any degree of confidence. And yet as the late Arnold Wolfers has cogently stated:

> As soon as one seeks to discover the place of goals in the means-ends chain of relationships, almost inevitably one is led to probe into the dark labyrinth of human motives, those internal springs of conscious and subconscious action which Morgenthau calls 'the most illusive of psychological data'. Yet if one fails to inquire why actors choose their goals, one is forced to operate in an atmo-sphere of such abstraction that nothing is revealed but the barest skeleton of the real world of international politics.[4]

To analyse the mechanism of value choices one may look mainly either for its causes, or probe into their intended results; one may concentrate upon the actors or upon the actions they are performing. The resulting studies of the motivations and intentions of the actors and of the causes and purposes of action inevitably overlap and hence it will suffice to sketch out what is involved in one of these approaches, namely the study of motivation.

As national interest is determined by individuals, it is reasonable to look into the way in which these individuals proceed in their personal affairs in order to see whether they behave similarly when formulating national interest.[5] Motivation of individual behaviour can be conceived in terms of needs: physiological, safety, love, esteem, self-actualization, preconditions of need satisfaction (e.g. freedom and justice) and the desire to know and understand. In each case motives arise in a number of these categories although the people are rarely conscious of them all. Their salience changes, e.g., an overwhelming concern with a physiological need which a person feels is threatened, may become his ultimate interest, but only temporarily; when it is reasonably satisfied, tension is directed to other needs. Thus tension shifts all the time. In theory, the number of motives or needs is endless as new ones are formulated as soon as others become substantially satisfied. Thus human attention incessantly wanders around, often suddenly changing direction. Periodically one interest, in whichever category it may lie, preoccupies the individual to the point of his neglecting other kinds of interests. It stands to reason that the individuals rarely, if ever, fully understand their own values, interests and motivations and that it is impossible to find fully rational criteria for their behaviour as a whole.

The motivations of decision makers acting on behalf of the state and, specifically, engaged in the formulation of national interest, can be analysed in similar terms. There is the same confusion of the categories of motives, values and needs, the eternal changes in their salience, the recurrent temporary preoccupation with some at the cost of neglecting others. Few rational criteria can be applied and, particularly in retrospect, it seems clear that basic interests are often neglected because peripheral ones happen to preoccupy the decision makers.

Motivation in the choices of values related to national interest is much more baffling than that in the behaviour of the individuals from which it differs in two significant respects. First, the parallel between national values, goals and interests and those of the individual is not complete and the dangers of pushing it too far are obvious. For instance, although such a parallel lies between the survival of the individual and the self-preservation of the state, it cannot be fully extended into the means of securing survival; whereas the individual's needs of food and drink are physiological and immutable, the state's needs of defence are social and cannot be regarded as immutable. More generally, the tendency to personalize the state and to compare its goals and needs with those of the individuals, if pushed too far, inevitably leads to confusion.

Second, an individual who decides for himself does not need to articulate his definitions and rarely, if ever, does so. National interest is determined by many individuals each of whom is concerned with persuading or at least informing others and this applies even to the most autocratic rulers. We have thus more explicit sources available to analyse choices of national interest than individual preferences but this material is often misleading and, moreover, unlike the behaviour of individuals, that of states cannot be studied under experimental conditions or compared with that of others in statistically significant terms.

Values

Values are such a fundamental notion that they defy definition by reference to other terms.[6] They describe the inner element brought by the decision makers to bear upon the processes of making decisions. It is analytically convenient although often empirically impossible to determine whether the values found in the formulation of a specific interest had been internalized by the decision makers or introduced only in response to environmental pressures, domestic or international.

Little agreement can be reached on the nature and the significance of this element and many overlapping and ill-defined terms are employed to denote it: ideologies, doctrines, values and valuations, utilities, policies, commitments, goals, objectives, purposes, ends, programmes, interests, the good, aims, principles, ethos, the way of life, etc., etc. Social taboos arising from the desire to preserve the national value system from cold rational scrutiny which would expose its inconsistencies and weaken its emotional impact, as well as the difficulties of analysis, inhibit our understanding.

An explanation rather than strict definition of the notion of 'values' is therefore all we can, at the moment, aspire to. We deviate little from common usage by following Professor David Easton in saying that values '. . . can be ultimately reduced to emotional responses conditioned by the individual's total life-experiences'.[7] Applying the distinction here made between the aspirational and the operational levels, we can distinguish between aspirational values which combine into a *vision of the good life*, meaning the state of affairs which a person would find most desirable, and operational *objectives* (*goals, ends*) for which he has to find *means* and to which he applies his *principles of behaviour*; these combine into *policies* or *programmes*.

'*Ideology*' is a term often applied to value systems, combining both aspirations and actual policy. The relevance of this term must be discussed at some length as a distinction is frequently made between a foreign policy based upon an ideology and one based upon self-interest; the former concentrates upon some general values whereas the latter is pragmatically concerned with specific interests and issues. As may well be expected, these two types of foreign policy are no more than ideal types which do not occur in the world in pure form. In the terms of this analysis of national interest, the difference can be, to some extent, explained by the varying emphasis upon either the aspirational aspects and the whole of the national interest, or the operational level and its single components. This emphasis varies not only from time to time and from place to place, but also from individual to individual. Instead of futilely arguing to which type a foreign policy really belongs, it is preferable to reject the dichotomy and to employ the ideological and the self-interest approaches not as complete and exclusive explanations or theories but as alternative models. The problem is then reduced to a scrutiny of the foreign policy with a view to finding *both* the ideological and the self-interest elements in it and to decide in what sort of a mixture they occur.

How indeterminate this distinction is for western states is best shown by the example of the United States where the ideological and the self-interest approaches alternate and mingle both in the academic discussion between the 'idealists' and the 'realists' and in actual policy behaviour. The shift was particularly pronounced at the end of the First World War when President Wilson's idealistic policy was replaced by a particularly narrow interpretation of self-interest. A similar but more gradual and less drastic shift is probably taking place now from the post-war policy, which centred upon a crusade against Communism, to one much more pragmatically oriented. Despite some ingenious speculations about the cyclical nature of such shifts, it is hard to believe that there is more substance in the theories advanced than in similar theories about trade cycles. It stands to reason that whenever incompatible considerations have to be taken into account, a policy based predominantly upon one of them must inevitably become one-sided so that a swing of the pendulum is required towards the opposed consideration. The length of the cycle and the violence of the swing are not, however, governed by natural or even historical laws although it is useful to be reminded that no policy can develop in a linear way indefinitely and that eventually a swing away from it will take place.

Some western scholars still argue among themselves as to the place of ideology in the foreign policies of the Soviet Union and China. Notwithstanding their controversies, it seems clear that all Communist decision makers are governed both by considerations of ideology and of political power and national self-interest. Some of them are, of course, more governed by the former and others more by the latter and therefore, as in the foreign policy of the United States, we can discover distinct fluctuations in Communist foreign policies which can be of great political significance. It is, however, unnecessary to prolong the arid controversies as to whether the predominantly ideological orientation of the Soviet Union is now being actually replaced by one of self-interest or whether such a trend is likely in China; whether their rulers are first and foremost Communists or Russians or Chinese nationalists. The two great Communist powers as well as individual leaders within them greatly differ in their priorities but it is safe to assume that all of them are concerned with their respective national interests and that they include in their definition both ideological and national power political elements.

The analysis of the policies of new states according to whether they emphasize ideology or self-interest often takes the form of distinguishing between ideology—and politics—and economics. In their first post-independence stage most new states were strongly motivated by the ideology of anti-imperialism (or anti-colonialism) which found its main expression in their fierce insistence upon complete independence from the ex-imperial power, especially if the latter had been reluctant to grant independence. This ideological orientation adversely affected the major economic interests of the new state as is well shown by the example of Indonesia. Eventually economic considerations tend to prevail and to alter the ideological emphasis of foreign policy. A similar fluctuation occurs in the policies of ex-colonies which started their independence on a friendly footing and hence under the influence of the ex-imperial power and which then became affected by the desire to assert their full independence.

8/Dichotomies and Choices

Some major problems of choice

The ultimate mystery of decisions which, in some cases at least, are clearly acts of free will and products of imagination, escape full explanation. No attempt is made here to try one.[1] After discussing some of the general problems of choice, the five sections of this chapter merely outline the issues of freedom and will, dynamism, attitudes to the domestic and the international environments and to conflict and co-operation.

Whenever a decision is made, competing values and alternative choices are considered; whenever from among others one option is decided upon, this *ipso facto* means that the other options are dropped. As much as all other decisions about foreign policy and, in fact, about human affairs in general, those about national interest invariably involve problems of choice between alternatives and frequently also incompatibilities and contradictions. Making a choice is a difficult and unpleasant task: some values must be neglected for the sake of others. It is, moreover, never quite certain that the choice will prove to be the right one or that it will escape stringent political criticism.

Hence the general human tendency to avoid difficult choices and immediate commitments through postponing decision. With the passage of time, either the position may become clarified as to which of the competing values should prevail or they may become reconciled in the form of a compromise. Tempting as procrastination is, it carries its dangers and it often proves untenable, at least in the long run. This is pithily expressed in the old adages about the impossibility of having the cake and eating it or about the dangers of sitting on the fence or of falling between two stools. The major danger of procrastination is that, with the lapse of time and the change in circumstances, the decision maker may lose his freedom of choice altogether as the options originally available gradually disappear. In the absence of alternatives, he may be eventually left with an outcome much less desirable than that of other originally possible courses of action.

Arguably, choice is affected by the differing ways in which the various states are culturally conditioned to tolerate incompatibilities. Thus western states could be expected to be influenced by the Aristotelian logic with its 'principle of the excluded middle' which, although it is not generally taught or directly referred to, forms the basis of all western thinking. The Marxist dialectical logic enables its supporters to accommodate incompatibilities by classifying them as thesis and antithesis, or short-range tactics against long-range strategy. New states seem unfettered in what to westerners sometimes appears their blithe ways of refusing to see the contradictions in their policies. All systems, however, fail to avoid contradictions. The confusions in the definition of the national interest of an ex-colony which is politically hostile to but economically dependent upon the ex-imperial power or a racialist neighbour, are matched by the contradictions between political and ideological hostility and a degree of economic and now also strategic co-operation between the two superpowers.

Once the choice is made by (or imposed upon) the decision maker, it invariably exercises a lingering effect on subsequent choices. First, the decision maker's image of the environment is sensitized to everything concerned with the option chosen and hence his sensitivity to anything related to alternatives becomes blunted. Second, he tends to adhere to his choice and to its consequences owing to the universal phenomenon of inertia,[2] both of his mind and of the bureaucratic machinery within which he operates. Although inertia frequently has the undesirable consequence of ossifying decisions long after they have lost their original justification, it is essential for the orderly functioning of the minds of the individuals as well as that of institutions. Persistent general rethinking and innovation are clearly beyond their capacities and in most specific cases they are difficult, costly and risky. It is a basically sound economic principle that change is not even considered as long as no distinct danger signals have arisen indicating that the original choice is wrong and has unwelcome effects. Even when a change is envisaged, inertia strongly favours the original decision as, in order to prevail, the benefits of a change which are, by their nature, speculative, must appear to be clearly greater than the cost of disturbance. There is thus a good reason why people tend to cling to their outworn definitions of national interest as much as they do to inadequate filing systems in their offices or to outworn and inefficient systems of central heating in their homes. All of these have to be on the point of breaking down or otherwise people must be offered very tempting alternatives before they contemplate change.

In many cases decision makers are perplexed by the overwhelming number of factors which should be taken into account; these include all the values and interests directly and indirectly involved as well as all the likely beneficial and also detrimental effects of the various options contemplated. In most controversies, the participants tend to concentrate upon some salient aspects and simply to ignore others, but as debate develops, the salience of arguments often shifts, showing that the criteria by which their relevance was chosen were either somewhat arbitrary or ephemeral or both. The constant fluctuations in the salience of arguments is well exemplified in the alternation between political/strategic and economic priorities determining British defence policy since the war, discussed in Chapter 4. Or to take specific issue of this policy, both government and opposition discussed the British presence east of Suez mainly from the strategic/military angle in the late 1950s but more from the political and economic angles in the later 1960s;

in the former period, defence considerations determined foreign policy, in the latter the order was reversed.

The Norwegian foreign minister, Halvard Lange, clearly articulated in June 1948 the main reasons swaying Norway in choosing between the grand alternatives of a regional Scandinavian and an Atlantic defence alignment:

> But nothing is gained by overlooking that the different experiences of our three countries during the war have created a different atmosphere regarding the attitude toward the main contemporary foreign policy questions in Norway, Sweden and Denmark . . . In addition there is a genuine difference in the strategic situation of our three countries. Both of these factors lead to dissimilarities in the evaluation of the risk factors we face in the present and the near future international situation, and a different appraisal of which way we ought to follow in order to meet the dangers we face . . .[3]

Mr. Lange was fortunate that the two fundamental elements he had singled out—recent historical experience and strategic location—both suggested the same choice, an Atlantic alignment, for Norway, and appeared to be sufficiently strong to prevail against counter-arguments for the Scandinavian alignment. There was no need for him to dwell upon the more controversial political and economic implications. His task would have been infinitely harder had the recent historical record indicated conclusions different from those indicated by Norway's strategic location.

Similarly in 1967 the British decision to withdraw from east of Suez was taken relatively smoothly against rather unexpectedly little opposition because the dominant economic arguments in favour of the withdrawal converged with political and purely strategic ones. The parallel decision to enter the European communities is not based on an equally solid consensus as the issue is much more complex and neither its economic nor its political aspects are clear; even if these get somewhat clarified, they could indicate opposite courses of action.

The perplexities of choice and even more so of the arguments about it are further enhanced whenever some vital arguments militate against the ideology and/or ingrained traditions of the country so that the decision makers dare not openly mention them and sometimes do not frankly and fully admit their existence even to themselves. For instance, it took a very long time for the two superpowers to articulate their interdependence in the prevention of a nuclear war and they are only now groping towards a clearer assessment of the meaning of the Sino-Soviet conflict in their relationship. Despite repeated declarations of protest, the Soviet Union has a vital interest in the continuing presence of the United States in central Europe as a means of preventing an uncontrolled revival of German militarism. Although in the past they had insisted upon the unrestricted freedom of travel through the Suez Canal, the Americans are grateful for the strategic consequences of its present closure which blocks easy Soviet access to the Persian Gulf and the Indian Ocean. Their commercial losses notwithstanding, the British also share this view. Even the vilified United States intervention in Vietnam is not completely unwelcome to the Communist powers —for the Chinese it means a diversion of American interest from the more central areas of Taiwan and Japan, for the Russians, a welcome diversion of their dangerous Chinese neighbour. Many further examples could be readily found.

Freedom and will

A fundamental problem confronting all those concerned with determining national interest is the degree of freedom they possess for the purpose. The traditional philosophical and theological arguments between the voluntarists and the determinists scarcely apply, as neither extreme position appeals to the modern mind. Spinoza's equation of freedom with rationality seems to be more relevant: '[Freedom is not] . . . an absolute freedom of the will but rather a relative freedom of intelligence'.[4] We are inclined to interpret necessity as the parameters of action imposed by the environment and freedom as the facility of making choices within these parameters. This ecologically interpreted freedom has been scrutinized by the various schools of thought among the geographers,[5] of which the 'environmental possibilists' adopt a position closest to the one here outlined.

The cultural traditions concerned with the freedom to act have great significance. Both the British and the Americans are traditionally inclined to have voluntarist attitudes to foreign policy. In contrast to the political thought on the Continent, which centred on the notions of necessity and of *raison d'état*, the two 'Anglo-Saxon' countries enjoyed a unique 'moral opportunity' in their exceptional safety based upon the combination of law, order and prosperity at home, together with security from foreign invasion provided by the Channel and the Atlantic respectively. Whereas Britain with her much more limited resources has been retreating from this position ever since the beginning of the century, the United States remained influenced by its 'myth of omnipotence' until the lessons of Soviet nuclear capability and of the post-war debacles in mainland China and now in Vietnam were fully realized.

The Soviet Communist doctrine leads to interpretations of freedom which fluctuate between Marx's inclination to 'fatal determinism' and Lenin's more voluntarist views. Actual Soviet foreign policy which seems to follow the perceived movements of 'the revolutionary wave' in the world, comes quite close to the ideas of the environmental possibilists. In the absence of sufficient analysis, it seems impossible to generalize about the position of new states except that they all seem reluctant to accept necessity and show the tendency to act in a more voluntarist fashion than do older states. It is by no means clear whether this generalization applies also to Communist China; in retrospect, the first two decades of her foreign policy may appear to be much more in the 'possibilist' tradition than they seemed to be at the time.

In a behavioural analysis of the freedom to act, it is convenient to distinguish between the domestic and the foreign environments; within each, the parameters of freedom are determined by the combination of two interconnected factors, capabilities and will or, as the strategists now say, intentions. To take the example of the two great expansionist interpreters of their respective national interests, Napoleon and Hitler, they were both capable of undertaking uniquely extensive military operations owing to the combination of great resources, good organization and social popularity at home together with the absence of matching resources or of will in other states. The international parameters were particularly loose in the interwar period owing to the disarmament, the economic disorganization and a weakening of political will in the West. The basic idea of the post-war containment has been to determine with greater rigidity and clarity the parameters of permissible action for would-be contenders for power.

The United States dilemma in Vietnam can be explained in terms of the parameters of freedom of action there being quickly narrowed by the combination of the growing unpopularity of the war at home and the stubborn unbroken resistance in the field. The case of Vietnam illustrates the crucial importance of the men or man in power in interpreting the parameters: the major criticisms of President Johnson were that he was too slow in deciding that withdrawal from Vietnam was becoming imperative. Neville Chamberlain in the late 1930s pursued his policy of appeasement not only because he was hopeful of Hitler's ultimately peaceful intentions but also because he believed, perhaps erroneously, that the British public would reject the substantial rearmament deemed essential for a firmer policy. The decisive role played by key decision makers is best illustrated by the contrast between the Czech and the Polish leaders before the outbreak of the Second World War. The former gave in to Hitler's demands in 1938 although the Czech forces were strong enough to oppose the Nazis for a few weeks on their own and could hope for subsequent outside support; the latter opposed similar demands in 1939 although the German forces were very much stronger in relation to theirs and the international support, though promised, could scarcely be expected to be effective.

The domestic and foreign parameters of freedom may come so close as to leave no room for manoeuvre. Nevertheless, states and statesmen always retain what may be called 'the suicidal alternative' and, by trying to do what seems to them impossible, they sometimes perish but sometimes achieve what they want. The North Vietnamese struggle against the United States and perhaps that of the Israelis against the Arabs can be quoted as examples of success; success would have been likely for Czech resistance to Hitler in 1938. The interpretation of the limits to the freedom to act is based on attitudes to the taking of risks which seem to be more closely connected with the power status and capabilities than with the ideology of a state. The changes in the international behaviour of the Soviet Union since she has reached a degree of nuclear balance and of economic advancement when contrasted with the propensity to take risks among new states indicates that the higher the power status and the greater the capabilities, the less has the state the need to take risks and the more it becomes unwilling to take them to avoid jeopardizing what it already has.[7]

Freedom can be described as the capacity to decide for oneself rather than depend upon decisions made by others, as well as the capacity to be active and not only reactive. Here the major role has been traditionally played by power. It is clear that it is ultimately the superpowers which decide matters of nuclear strategy and ultimately the issue of nuclear peace or war; other states have varying degrees of influence upon each superpower but this influence is in all cases extremely limited. Likewise the future of the Scandinavian countries clearly depends upon the decisions of the Six and of Britain on which they have precious little influence. An Israeli diplomat comparing the position of his country with that of a middle power such as Britain can have few doubts that the freedom of the two is of a different order.[8]

The correlation between power and freedom is, however, by no means absolute and, in fact, it appears to be waning. First, the correlation is largely limited to the operational level at which small states come up against the opposed wills of the great powers which, being backed by superior capabilities, usually prevail. There is no such limitation regarding aspirations which can be determined in an absolute fashion. Second, the freedom of movement of the superpowers is now severely curbed by the restraints of nuclear deterrence; in fact, they are in some, though not all respects, much more restricted in the application of force than are small states. This curb on the behaviour of the states endowed with the greatest resources is reinforced by a more general restraint imposed by the public debates in the United Nations. Together they allow an unprecedented degree of stability and of freedom of manoeuvre to small states. This freedom remains, however, limited: it has allowed Fidel Castro to defy the United States but has proved insufficient to allow the Czechs to operate a liberal Communist regime which was unacceptable to the Soviet Union.

Dynamism

Dynamism is undoubtedly a crucial feature of any definition of national interest although it is extremely hard to conceptualize it and, even more so, to seek promising empirical indices for its analysis. For instance, a difference in dynamism seems to be the major differentiating factor between post-war Britain and Germany, Japan or France. Dynamism, being a desire to change, inevitably stems from some disequilibria or tensions, be they between the aspirations and the actual policies and/or capabilities, or between either and the international environment. To use Toynbee's concept of challenge, a dynamic conception of national interest arises in conditions where tensions are sufficiently powerful to avoid stagnation but insufficiently powerful to cause disintegration. They were in differing degrees right both for the two defeated powers and for France which had been humiliated and occupied during the war. All the three countries could not expect much and felt the strong desire to survive and to rehabilitate themselves; moreover, they were offered the opportunity and the outside assistance to do so. By contrast, post-war Britain, having won the war at a colossal cost, felt the need and full justification for relaxing after the war; failing an adequate challenge, the British conception of national interest was relatively static as manifested in her slow economic growth and indecisive and ineffective foreign policy.

Dynamism in determining national interest is governed by the attitudes taken to the dichotomies of stability and change, inflexibility and flexibility, conservatism and innovation, support for the *status quo* and revisionism. Although these pairs of dichotomies overlap, they do not do so completely. It is well worth investigating their interrelationship as some misconceptions can arise from it.

One can hypothesize with a fair degree of confidence that national interest is stable when its major stress is on aspirations more than upon the operational level as this makes it less sensitive to changes in the environment and in the net achievement capability. Stability is strongly enhanced by the sheer lapse of time which tends to endow accepted definitions with an aura of tradition and to smooth out some of their problems and contradictions, by the continuity of government and of a powerful civil service and by a stable net achievement capability. Instability is induced by the absence of any of these elements. It seems plausible that instability in the definition of the interest is basically caused by excessive tension between the aspirational and the operational levels as well as by clashes between single interests. This tension may be inherent in the uncoordinated nature of the current definition but may be also caused by changes either in values and outlooks or within the environment or in the resources commanded so that the net achievement capability is out of balance with the goals pursued. It is also likely that central interests which are regarded as vital would be stabler whereas interests regarded as peripheral would be more volatile.

As it is obviously relevant for international interaction to estimate how stable the conception of national interest is likely to prove, we can attempt to rank stability within the main groups of states, using different bases of stability:

1 Determination by length of *tradition*:

West   Communist   New

STABLE   UNSTABLE

2 Determination by *ideology*:

Communist   West   New

STABLE   UNSTABLE

3 Determination by *rationality and logic*:

West   Communist   New

STABLE   UNSTABLE

On the surface of it, a stable definition is likely to prove rather inflexible whereas an unstable one is likely to be more flexible. In fact, this correlation is not necessarily true. A stable definition of national interest need not be devoid of flexibility nor is a volatile one *ipso facto* flexible. On the contrary, it is conceivable that an orderly, stable definition would allow a clearer perception of the needs for adjustment and the adjustments deemed

5

necessary may be made more readily than on a less stable basis.

Much closer is the correlation between stability and conservatism; indeed, it is difficult to conceive of a substantial degree of conservatism without a stable base. There are several converging reasons why conservatism which, in turn, is conducive to stability, holds a natural appeal. They are found in the limitations of human brain power; the cost of innovation and even of a serious 'feasibility study' of change; the doubts inherent in forecasting the success of change; the inertia of bureaucratic machineries and of international relationships. If innovation is the opposite of conservatism, readiness for it should depend upon the degree of instability. Stability and conservatism are not, however, fully correlated. As has been argued, it is in stable rather than unstable systems that we find the decision makers flexible, i.e. open to innovation. In unstable systems, however, decision makers find it hard to be truly conservative as this requires a successful and preferably long tradition.

A conservative definition of national interest is not tantamount to a conservative attitude to the international environment which takes the expression of support for the *status quo*. This is the case only with the 'have' states whose national interests are reasonably satisfied and which harbour no serious grievances against the international system. A 'have not', a state which feels seriously thwarted in the pursuit of its national interests, is bound to favour a revisionist policy aiming at the adjustment of the unsatisfactory international system; if it defines its national interest in a conservative manner and keeps it stable, it is likely merely to persevere in its revisionist attitudes.

Domestic and international choices

Although the meaning of the domestic-foreign divisions has been already touched upon in Chapter 1,[9] the problems of choice within each environment and, even more so, between the two, are so fundamental that they are separately discussed in this section. These problems can be grouped into three major categories: choice of goals within the domestic environment, choice of goals within the international environment and the relationship between the two or, as it is now often called, the problem of 'linkage'. The last mentioned group of issues is by far the most complex and obscure one. It has not yet been sufficiently explored probably because the intimate fusion of domestic and international matters has taken place only recently and our categories and modes of thinking stem from previous generations when the two domains were more clearly separated.

The choices of goals within each environment are relatively much simpler. Despite the enormous variety of the choices people make and the priorities they accord, it is impossible to deny that all societies experience and have to satisfy certain basic needs; this is the area of necessity beyond which choice becomes voluntary. What is unclear and is frequently hotly disputed, is the exact extent of this necessity. Within the domestic environment every society has to satisfy some basic needs of economic resources, social order and cultural needs. The definition of these basic needs varies not only from society to society but within each society. In most cases, however, we find a hard core of the essentials on which a basic social consensus exists. The remainder is subject to political argument in which competing groups and views clash. 'Authoritative allocation of values' can therefore be considered as the essential function of government; the form of the political argument over this allocation and the number and nature of the groups taking part in it are the major features distinguishing one political system from another. Societies in which no such hard core of agreement is found, lack the basic consensus for their perpetuation and are accordingly unstable. In our generation their continued existence is often ensured by the operation of the international system but, in the longer run, it cannot be taken for granted.

The hard core of necessity in the choice of goals in the international environment consists of survival, the self-perpetuation of the state and its security; its traditional instrumental goals are concerned with power, especially military power. An increasing stress is now being laid upon international co-operation as a more promising method of ensuring the security of the state and also one suitable for satisfying an increasing range of other, non-security interests which can be met domestically only less efficiently and at a higher cost, or sometimes cannot be satisfied at all. Moreover, increasing although so far small and uninfluential numbers of individuals refuse to continue defining all the major social goals within the circumscribed boundaries of a national interest.[10] However, at the level at which actual decisions about the national interest are ultimately made, the traditional mode persists.

Even at the level of their minimum definition, the essential domestic and international goals can occasionally confront the decision makers with irreconcilable demands. The position is aggravated by the ill-defined nature of these minima so that the decision makers find themselves in the proverbial situation of being ground between two mill-stones: neglect of domestic pressures and priorities incurs the penalty of an electoral defeat or, in more authoritarian regimes, of a popular rising; neglect of international pressures and needs can result in the obliteration of the state.

Whereas in the past continental states recognized necessity and accorded primacy to foreign policy, in their relative isolation and safety, Britain and the United States gave priority to domestic politics. Post-war events have blurred this traditional distinction but its implicit assumption is still valid: it seems true that, as far as they deem it possible, decision makers in all political systems prefer to concentrate upon and to give priority to the domestic environment and to full control over things; they have to be forced by irresistible pressures to accord priority to the international environment and to accept only limited influence over things. What is involved in the choices has been analysed by the late Professor Arnold Wolfers by making the telling distinction between 'possession goals' and 'milieu goals'.[11]

The essence of the possession goals is to enhance or preserve things to which the state attaches value; they may be as different as control of a territory, membership of the Security Council or tariff preferences. Their main characteristic is found in their competitive nature: the state demands that its share of certain values which are in limited supply is preserved or increased which, inevitably, is at the cost of others. To use the terminology of the theory of games, possession goals are based upon a model of international politics as a 'zero sum game' in which the gain of one party is inevitably at the cost of the others.

The essence of the milieu goals is that they do not involve the defence or the increase of possessions held to the exclusion of others but aim at shaping the conditions in the international environment, beyond the boundaries of the state within which it enjoys a relatively absolute power. The main characteristic of this class of goals is that they are co-operative and not competitive, that they are achieved not at the cost but to the joint benefit of others. They are based upon a model of international politics as a 'non-zero sum game' in which co-operation increases the pay-off so that all are better off (although not necessarily to the same extent).

One of the recurrent gross oversimplifications in the debates on national interest is the stark counter-position of the two classes of goals. Possession goals are often regarded as being the only ones truly in the national interest—by the chauvinists, because they are concerned with exclusive national possessions, by the internationalists, because they indicate what to them is a reprehensible spirit of national selfishness and acquisitiveness. Goals not directly concerned with the possessions of the state are always suspect. The very word 'international' means that goals may be understood that are not really in the national interest or that the government can or should pursue goals other than those concerning this interest. This is the reason why Professor Wolfers coined the emotionally neutral term of 'milieu' goals.

The traditional preference for possession goals may be justly considered as the manifestation of a general *spiritus dominandi*, of the inherent tendency of states to replace the uncertainties of being dependent upon the conditions prevailing in their international environment and the wills of other states by the relative certainty of having things under their own control. Although official spokesmen of all states have repeatedly been on record registering their beliefs in the interdependence of states and the value they attach to the milieu goals, not only do their actions often belie their stated convictions but the suspicion lingers that in many cases even their aspirations remain atavistically connected with possession goals.

In fact, milieu goals need not be regarded as being unconnected with, or even directly opposed to, national interest—as may sometimes appear the case when they are opposed to the traditional notions of national security and military preparedness. The creation of a better international system to live in is not only desirable but has become indispensable for the national interest of all states as the present system presents them much too starkly with the dangers of violent conflicts and of nuclear war. The trouble with the milieu goals is not that they are not in the national interest but that they are so hard to achieve as they depend not upon the efforts of a single state but also upon the concerted wills of others.

Conflict, co-operation and power

Parallel and overlapping with the distinction between possession and milieu goals is a distinction based upon the two modes of international interaction, conflict and co-operation. If a state concentrates upon possession goals, inevitably it is drawn into conflict with other states whose wills it must overcome; if it concentrates upon milieu goals, it must secure the co-operation of other states without which the goals become unattainable. The suspicion of milieu goals extends to that of co-operation which, in its extreme formulation, jeopardizes the security and the military preparedness of the state and, therefore, is some-times said to be not in the national interest. In fact, the dilemmas of choice are often acute. The more a state concentrates upon the conflict types of interaction, the less chance has it to develop co-operation. The more it concentrates upon co-operation and, to encourage it, reduces its preparedness for acute conflict and for countering violence, the more it incapacitates itself for facing possible dire contingencies. No statesman can accept the stark dichotomy between the mode of conflict which is characteristic of the past systems of power politics and that of co-operation which is supposed to characterize the brighter future ahead. In the choice of his goals and of the means for their pursuit he is constantly forced to compromise, to choose a combination of the two modes which, however, can significantly vary from nation to nation and, within each, from individual to individual.[12]

The general attitudes adopted to conflict and co-operation give the decision makers a general sense of direction when they are faced with specific issues. They decide according to how much value they attach to the principle of co-operation as well as to the various kinds of co-operation and to how much risk they are willing to take to wage conflicts in general and in their various forms. Needless to say, this general sense of direction falls far short of a complete and reliable guide to a specific deci-sion. A short-cut constantly employed to avoid the obvious difficulties of carefully weighing the pros and cons of each issue is to form generally conceived relationships of friendship or hostility which to a large extent predetermine the mode of inter-action on all the issues which may arise. This short-cut carries its own dangers and dilemmas and merely simplifies the decision makers' task.

When a state in its interaction with another state is fully governed by their basic relationship, it becomes inflexible in determining single issues. The image of a trusted friend with whom conflict is unthinkable tends to become one of an ally who must not be antagonized; major differences of interest which do not fit into the basic relationship can become obscured. Before alliances ultimately break down, sometimes for quite a while the obsolescent alignment prevents the state from pressing such interests as do not fit into the framework of the alliance. In the post-war world this phenomenon is illustrated by the gradual divergence of interests in the West where the alliance is based upon a common apprehension of the Soviet intentions, as well as in Eastern Europe where, apart from Soviet power, the states are linked by the common apprehension of Germany, and in a more remote way, of the United States. Instead of trying to accommodate their respective national interests to those of the leading superpowers with whom all are involved in the Cold War, over the last few years the single states have started questioning the assumption of basic congruence and pursuing their individual national interests which sometimes brings them into conflict with their superpower protector.

One can scarcely generalize about the value decision makers attach to actual relationships of friendship or about the intensity or permanence of images of friendship and of hostility. For instance, what meaning can the 'special relationship' retain considering the discrepancy in the contributions the United States and the United Kingdom can make to each other? Can United States-Soviet differences be forgotten, perhaps on the basis of the common apprehension of China, as have been the differences between France and Germany?

The expectations of the other state's behaviour which are the crucial factor determining one's own actions, vary from state to state and from case to case. Thus the United States has been acting on the basis of the image of China which anticipated much more hostile behaviour than the images held by the majority of its western allies. This image may be undergoing some change now. The Eastern European Communist regimes, although genuinely supported by the Soviet Union which put them into power, have been taught by history to expect a fair degree of conflict in their relationship with the Union. By contrast, the western allies expect so much from their relationship with the United States that quite frequently the actual behaviour of the Americans necessarily proves disappointing. The world does not neatly divide into heroes and villains, into 'peace-loving' and 'aggressive' states. The traditional distinction between the *status quo* states being peace-loving and the revisionist or expansionist states being aggressive, holds little appeal for the world today which is in the throes of change. To the majority of states, the preservation of some aspects of the existing order, e.g. of the remaining vestiges of the colonial system, appears as the starkest form of conflict behaviour.

The degree of stress upon conflict or co-operation in the definition of the national interest has a decisive influence upon the state's attitudes to power, especially military power. Obviously, stress upon conflict raises expectations of its arising and hence the propensity to devote more attention to the accumulation of power, especially military power, either through the development of appropriate military capabilities within the states or through securing suitable and adequate allies. Stress upon co-operation, by contrast, increases the tendency to examine the implications of one's national interest with a view to adjusting it, whenever necessary and profitable, and to concentrate upon the non-military means of influence and instruments of state policy.

It is possible to detect here a degree of circularity. Undoubtedly the possession of military capabilities tends to increase the propensity to conflict behaviour as the possession of these capabilities is invariably taken into account in international interaction. Violent conflict becomes more likely, whether the state possessing military capabilities is pressing its demands on another state, or resisting such demands. On the other hand, a state devoid of military capabilities is much more likely to favour co-operative behaviour, lacking as it does the means for succeeding in conflicts, especially if they involve the use of force. This relatively straightforward relationship of the past is becoming increasingly complex owing to the growing restraints emanating from the international environment. It certainly is now generally accepted that disarmament is scarcely likely to provide a helpful start in decreasing international tensions, as was widely believed in the 1920s. It seems to us much more likely that disarmament will follow, rather than precede, a political détente. Nevertheless, it is still acknowledged as a significant and symbolically central aspect of a political détente and hence the nuclear disarmament talks play such a prominent part in the evolution of the Cold War.

There seems to be no clear evidence that, if a state is a member of any of the three major contemporary groupings, it is automatically prone to resort to conflict and to concentrate upon possession goals. With some justification, all the three groups have been accused of conflict behaviour where co-operative behaviour may have served better; all of them seek some co-operation and pursue some milieu goals, although these differ in their extent and definition. The two major differentiating features regarding the propensity to possession goals and conflict seem to be satisfaction with the *status quo* and the power of the state. States which are satisfied with it have less cause to engage in conflict although this can arise if they stubbornly cling to their share of possession goals coveted by others, as exemplified in the dogged conflicts of the last defenders of the colonial systems. States which lack power have not the wherewithal to pursue any conflict behaviour to the point of using violence. It is the combination of dissatisfaction and power which is dangerous; at present it is epitomized in Communist China.

Part III

National Interest in Perspective

9/Towards an Assessment

Clarity of perception

With a subject of this nature, it would be impracticable to attempt a summary and conclusion of the book in the customary way. The argument is much too condensed to allow a meaningful brief summary; so many conclusions could be drawn from it that any selected by the author may strike the readers as idiosyncratic and arbitrary. The task of forming conclusions as to the nature of the concept will then be left to the individual reader who can, if necessary, easily refresh his memory of the argument by looking again through the whole book which is, after all, quite short. This chapter will merely attempt to get the subject into a broader perspective by discussing the issues of the clarity of perception of national interest, of its rationality and of its relationship with inter- and supranational values. These should be helpful both when applying the scheme to the analysis of the national interest of a specific single state and when looking for some general conclusions.

All those concerned with thinking about national interest or any other difficult and confused matter, should at an early stage of their research decide upon their strategy. To employ the distinction made between the aspirational and the operational levels, anybody endeavouring to distil the notion of national interest from the confused welter of foreign policy activities and of the relevant domestic and international issues and events, must decide how far he *would like* to go in his search for clarity and precision and also how far he *intends* to go despite the costs, delays and other obstacles he is likely to encounter. The scholar's desire for precision is probably much greater than that of a politician but both have to come to terms with the intractable nature of their subject and accept the fact that precision will almost certainly fall short of what they desire, and that looking for it is rather costly.

In each individual state national interest is likely to be perceived in a different manner and with a differing degree of clarity. Before determining the approximate amount of effort we wish to put into analysing it, it is well worth while to investigate briefly how clear the idiosyncratic national perception is likely to be when compared with the clarity of perception in other nations. Thus we may get at least an intimation as to what extent the ambiguities and uncertainties encountered are inherent in the national outlook and hence have to be accepted as a datum, or may be due to our lack of understanding and hence require research. Even a vague hypothesis about the characteristics which are conducive to clarity or lack of clarity of perception of national interest can have interesting heuristic uses. If the presence of certain features in national politics makes us expect a certain degree of clarity of definition of national interest, also vice versa, a certain degree of clarity of definition makes us expect the presence of some of these correlated features in national politics. If we encounter a discrepancy, we are likely to strike some significant problems.

Some major factors which are likely to confuse the perception of national interest have been touched upon in different contexts in the preceding analysis. The major domestic factors are: contradictions within the value system, whether between aspirations and actual policies or among single interests; disturbances in the value component such as a breakdown of political traditions, low degree of political consensus, inability to compromise on strong ideological principles, etc.; disturbances in the net achievement capability. The major international factors can be sought in the intractable nature of the international environment, especially when a state cannot comprehend or control it, e.g. when it cannot keep pace with technological change or when it relies heavily upon an alliance the *raison d'être* of which has disappeared; when it consistently fails to realize its values and to attain its objectives.

A clear perception of national interest is likely when conditions are the very opposite—stability of values and of the net achievement capability at home and a relatively comprehensible and manageable international environment. Possible additional factors are national unity in backing the existing regime, whether in its traditional form or when personified by a popular charismatic leader. This is particularly likely when one interest or strand of national interest is clearly salient, such as defence of the realm against a would-be aggressor, or unification of a nation scattered in several states. Possibly we may find a rather frequent correlation between the clarity of national interest and revisionist ideas as these have to be articulated whereas conservative support for the *status quo* requires no clear sense of purpose and may breed indifference to foreign policy and to the meaning of national interest.

Finally, to what extent are we right in thinking that perceptions of national interest are more blurred now than they used to be in the past? This impression is probably not entirely due to our lack of historical perspective. Political debates are now much more frequent and the arguments advanced in them more elaborate but confusion is caused by the convergence of several factors. The domestic reasons are both procedural and substantive: the greatly increased complexity of the decision-making machinery as well as the abandonment of the simple equation of national interest with national security. The obvious international reasons are the growing interdependence as well as the complexity of the world. Statesmen are acutely aware that they must pay increased attention to the international environment and try to manipulate it to suit their needs but they are also aware that they are unlikely to succeed because of the opposing wills of other states. This is conducive to indecisiveness, not only among the small and relatively powerless states but also among the great powers.

Rationality

The rationality of political decisions is highly suspect as even the most cursory analysis reveals a high incidence of non-rational, emotive elements, of sheer stupidity and of chance. Nevertheless it is a recurrent notion in political argument, both in terms of praise and of opprobrium; some political evaluations are directly centred upon it, most of them at least refer to it. A statement that an interest is 'rational' or 'irrational' need not be fully meaningless but on the whole it is the accepted way of arguing about our political likes and dislikes.

To begin with, it must be pointed out that the concept does not readily apply to the value-elements of decisions as no rational principle can indicate more than the processes by which we should choose our value priorities; the priorities themselves are, by definition, determined by non-rational methods. Regarding the formation of images on which decisions are based, rational principles are again helpful only with the procedures—by enabling us to assess how much information it is economic to collect, how it should be interpreted and whether the facts corroborate or falsify our assumptions.

Rational principles are most effectively applied to the ends-means relationship, to determine the choice of the most appropriate and economic means. Even this task is by no means straightforward. One can never be quite sure about one's assessment of the effectiveness and the cost of the means chosen. Moreover, values are attached not to the ends alone but also to the competing methods for their achievement and they completely escape rational evaluation. We cannot therefore hope to reach clear conclusions about the choices of means as one can when comparing competing methods for achieving an economic goal, as long as we confine ourselves to the economic costs and benefits and omit all other social considerations. We may at least discover that some means are less likely to achieve our ends than others and that some are quite unlikely to do so. Even then, although in the ends-means context an interest could be termed irrational, in the sense that it cannot or is very unlikely to be achieved, it still may be well worth pursuing, or at least aspiring to. Even if the 'interest' is no more than a grand myth, it still can be helpful in providing the nation with a sense of purpose. The nation may achieve more by falling short of this grand design than in setting its sights lower, on more easily achieved objectives; at least it will maintain the desired sense of direction. It may, of course, be dangerously deflected from achievable tasks.

Moreover, even in connection with the ends-means nexus, rational processes are not the only ones by which we are governed. They have to compete with emotions which must be legitimately taken into account because of their decisive role in value choices; they are circumscribed by the influence of tradition and inertia, which have already been discussed;[1] they are often ignored when states simply imitate other states, especially great powers and successful rivals. In every generation, irrational patterns of international behaviour are set this way. During the heyday of French influence even the pettiest of European rulers tried to emulate the court of Versailles; today even the pettiest states show a craving to operate the most sophisticated and expensive modern weapons system, usually at the cost of operational efficiency, while nuclear weapons have become a hallmark of great powers. Up to a point it is, of course, rational to provide oneself with what one's rival has, but the keeping up with the Joneses can be ruinous indeed.

This argument about the limited application of rational criteria to the definition of national interest is well illustrated by an example drawn from the politics of Australia, a country which justifiably is not regarded as less rational than most others. Although geographically Australia is part of Asia rather than of any other region and although many Australians have clearly realized it for a long time, until the Second World War her policy was based on an assumption that, under the protection of the British navy, she would manage to isolate herself from Asia

6

and maintain her western ways of life and her high standards of living by excluding Asian immigrants under the 'White Australia' policy. After the shock of the fall of Singapore which exploded the myth of an effective British protection, the United States became Australia's protector, but the growing impact of Asian states upon world affairs, the rise of Communist China and, since 1969, the impending revision of the American commitment to Asia, rendered the exclusive Australian policy increasingly more precarious. The policy has been subjected to re-thinking but, in the eyes of its liberal critics, its revision has been too slow and too slight. Rational arguments about the political costs incurred, and the unlikely success of any means open to continue the policy, were advanced and discussed. They were insufficiently compelling to prevail against the emotional attachment to the western ways of life, the wishful thinking that the policy may after all have a chance of success, especially if slightly modified to make it less offensive to the Asians, and also the unpromising example of all other multi-racial societies all of which have been faced with intercommunal troubles.

The concept of rationality becomes additionally misleading when applied to non-western cultures. To westerners in general terms, rationality means the process of finding a balance between the values held and the environment or, as Walter Lippman said, between desires and possibilities. Non-westerners hold, however, different values, specifically they tend to accord lower priorities to economic utilities. Hence the logic of the Arabs refusing negotiations with the Israelis as they consider it a humiliation, or of the ex-colonials who sometimes rejected the economic benefits of aid from and trade with an 'imperialist' state. Some critics of Communist regimes, especially of the Chinese, have questioned Communist rationality altogether. It is arguable, although not self-evident or necessarily convincing, that the Communists not only aspire to, but actively pursue, the values stated in a rigid way by the Marxist theory. Instead of scrutinizing the environment for constraints, as is done by others in search of optimal national interest, they often seem to concentrate upon increased organizational vigour and greater doctrinal fanaticism.

One important contemporary trend in the perennial argument about rationality is to equate it with precision and quantification, to concentrate upon the assessment of the suitability of means for ends and on the estimate of costs. However, even if we concentrate upon the choice of instruments and options within the limited context of a single issue or policy, we soon discover how fallacious it is to rely on purely economic or other relatively simple calculations. To take examples from the United States, it soon became obvious how crude and unsteady were the analysis of cost effectiveness in the simple form of asking for 'more bang for a buck' or the simple equation between military power and political influence. Nevertheless, despite strenuous efforts, the Americans seem incapable of making much progress in refining the criteria to make them politically useful. In Britain the problems of quantification were demonstrated by some critics of the governmental decisions to withdraw from East of Suez who explained it by juxtaposing the costs of the British presence and those of the National Health prescriptions. Turning aspirations to actual policies invariably involves a cost but cost is the only quantifiable aspect of foreign policy and the recurrent attempts to draw broader conclusions from it are dangerously misleading. Although it is essential to know the cost of specific policies, this knowledge is by no means tantamount to knowing whether the policy is worth while; the latter can be known only in the light of the value attached to the aspirations involved. The aspirations themselves completely escape any attempts at quantifications and no objective criteria can be agreed upon even for their ranking.

A degree of rationality can be infused into political argument if national interest is conceived in predominantly economic terms which enable us to use the monetary yardstick to compare and evaluate. Thus we tend to comment approvingly about the

apparent trend among new states to replace sentiments by calculations of national interest as the basis for their foreign
relations.[3]

Economic assessments are, however, incomplete. Economic
restraints and benefits, including marginal ones, were extensively analysed in the recent public debates in Britain about her
world role, her intention to join the European communities and
her proposed withdrawal from East of Suez. The debates have
not been in vain as they have helped to break down vague intuitive concepts into discrete elements which can be subjected to
further refinement and analysis. They were, however, inconclusive since no agreement could be reached upon the weighting of
the various elements and utilities and nobody could be quite
sure whether all the relevant elements had been noted. As in the
discussion of other composite concepts such as the *laissez faire*
idea of the general good, we must accept the limitations of the
idea that logically something general arises from the combination of single elements.

Intuitive definitions of national interests are justifiably suspect.
We associate them with traditionalism and resistance to
adaptation to new conditions, with autocratic systems and with
low political sophistication, with lack of perspective while the
nation is immersed in a violent crisis (as in Vietnam) and with
disguised sectional interests.[4] Hence the popularity of the attempts
at more precise formulation is understandable. The value of
these attempts is, however, limited. We can probe into single
aspects and elements, we can destroy the more blatant and unacceptable rationalizations and thus raise the general level of
political argument and turn it in a direction deemed less politically undesirable. At the same time, however, the nature of national
interest precludes the possibility of a full rational definition.

Between autonomy and interdependence

It is the basic tenet of the international system that states
enjoy sovereignty, which means that they are completely auto-

nomous in shaping their foreign policies and in formulating their national interests. This autonomy can be circumscribed or even abandoned by an act of will—states can decide to merge in larger units of varying character; they can also be forced to do so.

Although in theory sovereignty is enjoyed in equal measure by all states—the Charter of the United Nations speaks about the 'sovereign equality' of all its members—in practice the substance of this sovereignty greatly differs. The spectrum is wide. At the one end, we find the superpowers which, although constrained by nuclear deterrence, are much freer to define their national interests than any other state; at the other end, we find a state such as Czechoslovakia in which a reformulation of the national interest is taking place in the shadow of the Soviet troops which have been stationed there since August, 1968. Purely formal powers are, however, of some importance even if their substance is very slight. This is well demonstrated by the completely different political evolution of the Baltic states which have been formally incorporated in the Soviet Union since the end of the Second World War, and the Eastern European states which have not. Admittedly only within severe limitations and only sporadically, the latter, especially Rumania, have managed to assert a degree of autonomy in deciding for themselves as the others never did.

The major variable in the extent of autonomy seems to lie in the capabilities of a state. A powerful state is relatively immune from imperious intervention by others, is more self-sufficient and is less inclined to imitate other states. The other major variable is political will and readiness to take risks.

It is hard to find suitable indices for autonomy, since superficially identical phenomena acquire different meanings within different contexts. Thus, foreign troops on the territory of another state generally indicate lack of autonomy and their relative size can be used as a rough yardstick. This is the case of the Warsaw Pact countries or of South Vietnam. The growing emancipation of Japan's foreign policy correlates with the gradual removal of United States troops to fewer bases. In the Federal Republic of Germany a similar emancipation has taken place through the rapid growth of the German component of NATO to become the dominant contribution to NATO's land forces. Today the presence of foreign troops on German soil is only a marginal encroachment upon Germany's autonomy of decision; on the contrary, the Germans themselves think of it as a buttress which frees them from Soviet pressures and greatly oppose the recurrent proposals to reduce the foreign contingents.

When a foreign military base is located on national territory this likewise amounts to an infringement of autonomy, although on a lesser scale. However circumscribed the use of the base may be, its presence helps to ensure that the recipient state will not suddenly change its alignment. It is by no means a full guarantee as base agreements can be revoked and, as shown by the behaviour of Cuba, even their continued presence is not in all cases decisive in determining the recipient state's policy.

The traditional principle of sovereignty which plays a central role in the foreign policies of all states is now increasingly counteracted by the growing facts of interdependence which are being gradually shaped into a new, opposed principle. Although social needs continue to grow and require political action, an automatic corresponding increase in state activities and powers can no longer be taken for granted.

This slow and gradual but by now quite palpable shift away from the state to broader forms of social and political organization is caused by the dwindling of the state's net achievement capability, the combined effect of growing needs and of environmental pressures. The historically most important fields of activity must all be reconsidered. First, the traditional strategies of the single national states occasionally combining in alliances is being replaced by more permanent large coalitions. Second, in economics, the needs of international control have been recognized in the regulation of trade and are being accepted as indispensable also for the monetary system and discussed for aid and for the exploitation of natural resources. Third, the fantastic growth in social communication and in the mobility of individuals has broadened many cultural and social needs beyond the possibility of full satisfaction within the boundaries of single states. Finally, patriotism, the ideological base of the political coherence of states, is being threatened by a whole gamut of supernational ideologies—Communism, pan-Arabism, pan-Africanism, Europeanism, support for the United Nations, internationalism, etc.

The classical debate about state and society is reappearing in the new guise of a debate about state sovereignty and internationalism. Our generation will have to decide whether to give precedence to a nation whose needs are better satisfied in a broader political setting or to the state in its existing boundaries. The calculations are complex and a clear assessment is impossible but the principle of economy indicates that an increasing range of objectives can be achieved more cheaply and more efficiently internationally; also the ideological and ethical support for the nation state is somewhat weakening. Whereas in the past foreign policy was generally regarded as the handmaiden of domestic politics, and the maintenance of international order only an instrument to enable us to pursue undisturbed our domestic objectives, international order and peace are achieving an increasing momentum as ends in themselves and not as mere instrumentalities.

The behaviour of states is increasingly becoming what the sociologists sometimes call 'other-oriented'. Even within the old-fashioned alliances which were no more than extensions of the fighting power of single states, to make them effective in contemporary conditions, leaders are forced to define the objectives in a manner acceptable to others and account is taken of a sort of international consensus about what is morally permissible in international relations.

As intergovernmental co-operation of the traditional type is becoming more and more inadequate to overcome the limitations of the individual states in satisfying the growing range of social needs, some larger forms of political organization have to be considered. Unification of states through imperial domination seems now outdated, and even the tight federal patterns seem unsuitable for our generation as shown by the repeated unsucce.sful post-war attempts to apply them. All sorts of organizational forms have been devised and tried: global and regional, comprehensive and functional, intergovernmental and supranational. All international organizations have a dual role. The first and more pronounced function is to serve the interests of the individual members; if they fail to do so, the states refuse to join or leave them. The second, and so far lesser function, is to serve the international community which they embrace as a whole.[5]

International institutions have not replaced the individual states in their central role in the international system but they have greatly reduced the autonomy of these states in formulating their national interests. The additional constraints of international public opinion were never really effective in preventing sufficiently powerful states from doing what they thought to be in their vital interests. They are not effective now, either, but states take them more and more into account. As has been argued, the definition of interests as 'vital' is not based upon immutable objective criteria and some national decisions about matters that, in the past, would have been considered vital interests, bend to the criticism or even the anticipated criticism in the 'town meeting' of the world, the United Nations. This is particularly pronounced in the issues of colonialism.

The most significant development lies in the community elements which are being slowly introduced into state interaction, gradually transforming the traditional diplomatic bargaining and the log-rolling in international institutions. Although in practice the distinction between the community and the traditional methods is not nearly so clear-cut, in theory communal method means that the individual states confront one another not with their individual national interests which must be reconciled but rather with common problems to which they try to hammer out a communal solution. On a world-wide scale the progress in this direction has been marginal. The greatest successes of the United Nations have been on issues remote from the immediately vital interests of its members such as the concord on Antarctica or outer space. Progress has been greatest within the European communities until the crisis caused by President de Gaulle which ended in the so-called Luxembourg Compromise of 1965. Subsequently members reverted from the 'community method' to inter-governmental negotiations in which the community is only represented and in which the interests of the community as a whole are only one consideration which is often overridden in matters regarded as vital by the individual members.

Political integration is clearly one of the most important political phenomena of our age and it has therefore been subject to much analysis by political scientists. The process is usually conceived in the following stages: antagonism is reduced, co-operation replaces conflict, a common image of future conditions arises; it becomes increasingly less likely that members will choose objectives contrary to this image; priorities in foreign policy in general converge; the bargaining processes change under the impact of the community interest; eventually, on the basis of the gradually converging standards of evaluation, the communally accepted processes become a matter of routine.

So far the scope of the European communities has been limited, as foreign policy and defence matters do not come within it; moreover, the level of development of community sentiments is not very advanced as shown in the repeated crises of the community due to members reverting to more selfishly conceived notions of national interest. The devaluation of the franc decided upon in August 1969 without regard to the community is only the latest example. Despite these setbacks, undoubtedly the European Economic Community has instilled into its members a broader notion of self-interest and has encouraged even outsiders, such as Britain, to do likewise. Nevertheless, although the change to supranationalism is gradual and imperceptible, at some stage it will require a fundamental decision which may be beyond the capacity of the national goal-setting machineries as they now exist. The decision makers are all steeped in the traditions of power politics and feel that, although it may be inevitable that their automony in determining their respective national interests may be greatly circumscribed, they must retain the ultimate power of decision about what they think constitutes their hard core, about matters that are really vital. Only states which are much too small to be able to control their destinies, such as the three Benelux members, think favourably of supranationalism. When President de Gaulle obstructed the advance towards majority voting in the European Economic Community, this was not exactly a maverick act of an old-fashioned statesman; his attitudes are fully shared by many other Frenchmen, not to mention the British applicants. Even India, a state which prides itself on its international outlook, shows no inclination to abandon autonomy in vital matters. She has been persistently rejecting United Nations recommendations on Kashmir. Again in 1968, during the parliamentary debate about the nuclear non-proliferation treaty, Mrs. Gandhi, the prime minister, explicitly stated that India would be entirely governed by her national interest, although an enlightened one.[6] Ultimately, when an issue really affects them, all the states take a similar stand.

Thus, it appears that national interest is unlikely to disappear as a general organizing concept within the foreseeable future although the states will probably be increasingly circumscribed in the freedom of its definition. There is some hope that it may be interpreted in a more liberal and enlightened form. The prestige attaching to a state which has gained the reputation of acting unselfishly is likely to increase in an international system in which the traditional power elements are losing their dominant position. The claims of the individual states that they act to the benefit of humanity as a whole, protecting freedom or civilization or culture may be sheer hypocrisy or a mere rationalization, but when these claims are spread by the mass media they raise expectations which a state can disappoint only at its peril. Self-interest is by far a more important source of motivation than broader moral considerations. Nevertheless, self-interest can be enlightened. In 1907, Sir Eyre Crowe, in a famous memorandum, spoke about Britain harmonizing her foreign policy with the aspirations of other nations in order to avoid the 'natural fear and jealousy' attaching to her position as a dominant naval power. A similar reasoning may prevail with the dominant powers of our generation. The lesser powers would have to follow suit.

Notes
and
References

1/Meanings, History and Usages

1 See the bibliography in James N. Rosenau, "National Interest", *International Encyclopaedia of Social Sciences*, 1968.

2 Ibid., p. 34.

3 W. R. Schilling, "The Clarification of Ends—or, Which Interest Is National?", *World Politics*, 1956, pp. 567–8.

4 In *International Journal*, XXI, p. 194. See also Raymond Aron, *Peace and War*, 1966, p. 89.

5 D. Vital, *The Making of British Foreign Policy*, 1968, p. 11.

6 The Brookings Institution, *Major Problems of United States Foreign Policy 1953–1954*, 1955, pp. 373–5. See also F. Gross, *Foreign Policy Analysis* 1954, p. 53, and J. Frankel, *The Making of Foreign Policy*, 1967, pp. 54–6.

7 N. J. Padelford and G. A. Lincoln, *The Dynamics of International Politics*, 1962, p. 8.

8 In *International Journal*, XXI, 1967, p. 194. To a large extent the divergence between the two views can be explained as one between ends and means or aspirations and actual policies. (On the latter see Chapter 2.)

9 H. J. Morgenthau, *The Restoration of American Politics*, 1962, p. 199.

10 Cf. Charles A. Beard, *The Idea of National Interest: An Analytical Study of American Foreign Policy*, 1934, and James N. Rosenau, op. cit.

11 *The Times*, London, Oct. 9, 1968.

12 James N. Rosenau, op. cit., claims that national interest attracted attention as a tool of analysis rather late in history. This, however, was due to the general paucity of early analyses rather than to the inattention of the writers in the field.

13 F. R. C. Macridis (ed.), *Foreign Policy in World Politics*, 3rd edn., 1967; J. E. Black and K. W. Thompson, *Foreign Policies in a World of Change*, 1963; F. S. Northedge (ed.), *The Foreign Policies of the Powers*, 1968.

14 E.g. David Vital, *The Inequality of States*, 1967, defines as 'small states' those with populations under 10–15 million, when developed, and double that when not developed.

15 Cf. an outline of a five-way matrix in J. Frankel, *International Politics: Conflict and Harmony*, 1969, p. 14.

16 This is often assumed to be more important. Cf. B. Russell, *Principles of Social Reconstruction*, 1915 or A. Etzioni, *Active Society*, 1969.

17 See below, Ch. 2, pp. 31 ff.

18   Cf. A. M. Scott, *The Functioning of the International System*, 1967, pp. vii and 30.
19   A term coined by A. Wolfers and L. W. Martin in *The Anglo-American Tradition*, 1956.
20   Cf. A. B. Fox, *The Power of Small States: Diplomacy in World War II*, 1959.
21   The meaning of the concept is explained in the author's *The Making of Foreign Policy*, 1963 and 1967, Ch. 1.
22   Cf. J. D. Singer, preface to *Quantitative International Relations*, 1968, and in "Modern International War: from Conjecture to Explanation", in A. Lepavsky and others (eds), *Essays in Honor of Quincy Wright*, 1970.
23   Cf. J. D. Singer, "Modern International War: from Conjecture to Explanation", op. cit.

2/Analytical Distinctions and Theories

1   The British political system offers a good example in the Liberal Party which does not expect to form a government and hence is much freer to dwell upon aspirational interests than the other two parties, whether in government or in opposition. The history of the Labour Party offers clear examples of the fundamental change of emphasis from aspirational to operational interests whenever the party forms a government.

The Labour Party has institutionalized the representation of the aspirational and the operational interests within the party: whereas the Parliamentary Party and the National Executive Committee are concerned with the 'operational level' on which elections are fought, the annual conference represents 'the hopes and desires' of the rank and file while the left-wing members represent, in a sense, the party's 'social conscience'. (Cf. Austen Albu, "Should Labour Left Resign the Whip?", *The Times*, London, February 20, 1968.)

The distinction here made between aspirational and operational levels facilitates the reconciliation of conflicting views on the role of ideology in the Labour Party, represented in the writings of R. C. Mackenzie and S. H. Beer.

Similarly in the preface to *European Fascism*, pp. 2–3, J. S. Woolf notes that whenever fascist elements were included in right-wing authoritarian governments in Eastern and Central Europe, they became more concerned with operational interests and hence were more precise in their formulation than their counterparts in other countries where they did not participate in the government.

2   Cf. the analysis of Paul Seabury, *Power, Freedom and Diplomacy*.
3   This proposition pursues Arnold Toynbee's idea that challenge is the condition of the growth of a civilization, provided it is neither too severe nor too slight.
4   Lady Gwendolen Cecil, *Life of the Marquis of Salisbury*, Vol. II, p. 130 q. by J. Joll, *Britain and Europe*, 1950, p. 3.

5   Cf. Burton M. Sapin, *The Making of United States Foreign Policy*, 1966, pp. 98–9.
6   Cf. F. Schurman, *Ideology and Organization in Communist China*, 1966, p. 22.
7   M. Seliger, *Dimensions of Ideology*, mimeographed, 1968, passim, esp. p. 24.
8   *Power Through Purpose*, 1954. See also W. R. Schilling op. cit. in *World Politics*, 1956, pp. 573–4.

3/Theories of National Interest

1   Q. by W. J. Mackenzie, *Politics and Social Sciences*, 1967, p. 359, n. 2.
2   T. D. Weldon, *The Vocabulary of Politics* substituting 'national interest' for 'ownership'.
3   See below, pp. 67–72.
4   R. J. Rummel, "The Relations Between National Attributes and Foreign Conflict Behaviour", in J. D. Singer (ed.), *Quantitative International Relations*, 1968.
5   They began with Charles A. Beard, *The Idea of National Interest: An Analytical Study of American Foreign Policy*, 1934. See literature in Rosenau, op. cit.
6   The major theories have been grouped and summarized by Karl W. Deutsch in *The Nerves of Government*, 1963 and 1966, on whose account this section is based, and references to the relevant literature may be found there.
7   Cf. J. S. Hinsley, *Sovereignty*, 1966; J. Herz, *International Politics in the Nuclear Age*, 1959 and 1963; E. Cassirer, *The Myth of the State*, 1946.
8   For a selection of leading writings on the subject see J. Larus (ed.), *Comparative World Politics*, 1964, s. 3.
9   For further discussion see below Ch. 8.
10 The classical statement of the theory remains, H. J. Morgenthau, *Politics Among Nations*, 1st edn. 1948, 4th edn. 1967. See also G. Schwarzenberger, *Power Politics*, 1st edn. 1949, 3rd edn. 1966.
11 English translation, Weidenfeld and Nicolson, London 1967, Ch. 3, pp. 71–3.
12 Cf. A. Wolfers, "The Pole of Power and the Pole of Indifference", *Discord and Collaboration*, 1967; J. W. Burton, *International Relations: A General Theory*, 1965; J. Frankel, "Power Politics and Beyond", *Political Studies*, June 1966.

4/Dimensions of National Interest: I

1   J. D. Singer and M. Small, "Alliance Aggregation and the Onset of War: 1815–1945", in *Quantitative International Relations*, op. cit., pp. 247–8.
2   *War and Peace*, op. cit., Ch. III.
3   *Discord and Collaboration*, op. cit., pp. 73–7.

4 See ibid., pp. 68–70 and J. Frankel: *The Making of Foreign Policy*, op. cit., pp. 141–7.

5 S. S. Nilson, "Measurement and Models in the Study of Stability", *World Politics*, October 1967.

6 Cf. H. and M. Sprout, "The Dilemma of Rising Demands and Insufficient Resources", review article, *World Politics*, July 1968, and the literature there quoted.

7 G. Thompson, "Britain's Plan to Leave Asia", *Round Table*, April 1968, p. 118.

8 A. Baker-Fox, op. cit.

9 See above, p. 50.

10 See below, pp. 67–72.

11 Cf. David Vital: *The Inequality of States*, 1967, p. 118.

12 Cf. C. Wright Mills, *The Power Elite*, 1956.

13 B. G. Cohen, "Foreign Policy Makers and the Press", in James N. Rosenau (ed.), *International Politics and Foreign Policy*, 1967, pp. 223–5.

14 B. M. Sapin, *The Making of United States Foreign Policy*, 1966, p. 1.

15 Cf. R. N. Rosencrance: *Defence of the Realm*, 1968, pp. 271–2.

16 See D. Vital, op. cit., passim. esp. pp. 29–30.

17 A. Baker-Fox, op. cit., pp. 108, 114.

18 *Discourses*, Book 3, Ch. 2.

19 Cf. E. Weinthal and C. Bartlett, *Facing the Brink*, 1967, p. 216.

20 See below, Ch. 9.

5/Dimensions of National Interest: II

1 Cf. C. H. Commager, "A Limit to Presidential Power?", *The New Republic*, q. in *Survival*, July 1968, p. 128.

2 J. W. Burton, *Systems, States Diplomacy and Rules*, 1968, pp. 128–9.

3 Its existence is claimed by R. Ardrey, *The Territorial Imperative*, 1956.

4 Cf. J. Herz, *Foreign Policy in the Nuclear Age*, op. cit.

5 Quoted in A. Wohlstetter, "Strength, Interest, and New Technologies", *Adelphi Paper*, No. 46, 1967, p. 8.

6 Cf. H. and M. Sprout, *The Foundations of National Power*, 1945.

7 A term coined by François Perroux: see Wohlstetter, op. cit., p. 10.

8 Ibid., p. 8.

9 Cf. P. M. Burgess, *Elite Images and Foreign Policy Outcomes: a Study of Norway*, 1968, pp. 77, 143–4.

10 This does not prove, as is sometimes alleged, that Europe has lost its importance as a centre of world politics. On the contrary, it seems more plausible to assume that the two superpowers chose Asia for their confrontation for the opposite reason that they consider it as a peripheral area in which their interests are not as vital as in Europe. Korea and Vietnam rather than Germany became the testing ground in their local global competition not because they are more important, but because the lesser risks involved in them could be more readily faced.

11 See Sir Con O'Neill in *The Times*, London, July 26, 1968, and letters to the editor by Douglas Jay on 29th and by Sir Con on July 30, 1968.

12 E. Hambro, "Small States and a New League: from the Point of View of Norway", *American Political Science Review*, XXXVII, October 1943, p. 908, q. by P. M. Burgess, op. cit., p. 61.

13 Burgess, op. cit., Ch. 4.

14 A. G. Nasser, *Egypt's Liberation: the Philosophy of the Revolution*, 1956.

15 H. J. Morgenthau, *Dilemmas of Politics*, Chicago 1958, p. 48.

16 See discussion of 'vital interests' above, pp. 73–6.

6/The Structure of Decision Making

1 Cf. J. Frankel, *The Making of Foreign Policy*, op. cit.; on the United States which is the best documented political system, see B. M. Sapin, *The Making of United States Foreign Policy*, op. cit.

2 Cf. the argument about United States foreign policy by Sapin, op. cit., pp. 29–30.

3 Cf. K. W. Deutsch, *The Analysis of International Relations*, 1968, pp. 15–17.

4 For further analysis of the various stages of decision making see J. Frankel, *The Making of Foreign Policy*, Chs. 13–15.

5 Cf. the views of an Israeli ex-diplomat, David Vital, *The Inequality of States*, 1968, pp. 30–7 and *The Making Of British Foreign Policy*, 1969, passim., or *Political Quarterly*, July/September 1968.

6 For a general analysis of the agencies making foreign policy cf. J. Frankel, *The Making of Foreign Policy*, op. cit., Chs. 2 and 3.

7 In the sixties, opposition has become a fashionable topic of political analysis. For a lucid up-to-date survey of the field see G. Ionescu and I. de Madariaga, *Opposition*, 1968. Subsequent remarks heavily draw upon it.

8 *The Times*, London, September 23, 1968.

9 Cf. the precise formulation of the phenomenon by A. Downs, *An Economic Theory of Democracy*, 1957.

10 Max Beloff, *Foreign Policy and the Democratic Process*, 1955, pp. 73–4.

11 There are the Rand Corporation and the Hudson Institute. Proposals for an autonomous foundation for social sciences with direct access to the President have been made by Professor Marian P. Irish in A. A. Said (ed.), *Theory of International Relations*, 1968, pp. 154–9.

12 The most extensive account is found in A. Avtorkhanov, *Stalin and the Soviet Communist Party*, 1959.

13 Cf. Vital, op. cit., pp. 30–1.

14 Cf. J. Frankel, "Malaysia and Singapore in Interaction", *The Yearbook of World Affairs, 1970*.

15 Cf. Parker Moon, *Imperialism*, 1933.

7/Images, Motivation and Values

1 Cf. K. E. Boulding, *The Image*, 1956 and "National Images and

International Systems", *Journal of Conflict Resolution*, iii/2, June 1959. See also J. Frankel, op. cit., pp. 105–10.

2 Cf. the argument by D. MacLachlan, "Intelligence in Action", BBC Third Programme, April 22, 1968.

3 D. MacLachlan, op. cit.

4 A. Wolfers, op. cit., p. 70; Cf. also J. Frankel, op. cit., pp. 114–17.

5 A. H. Maslow, "A Dynamic Theory of Human Motivation", in Chalmers L. Stacey and Manford F. DeMartino (eds), *Understanding Human Motivation*, 1958, pp. 28 ff. q. by V. Van Dyke, "Value and Interest", *American Political Science Review*, 56, 1962, p. 569 ff.

6 For a comprehensive discussion of values in politics see A. Brecht, *Political Theory*, 1959, and D. Waldo, " 'Values' in Political Science Curriculum", in R. Young (ed.), *Approaches to the Study of Politics*, 1958. On values in foreign policy decisions see J. Frankel, op. cit., Chs. 8–10.

7 D. Easton, *The Political System*, 1953, p. 221.

8/Dichotomies and Choices

1 For a more detailed analysis of the problems of choice in foreign policy see J. Frankel, *The Making of Foreign Policy*, op. cit.

2 See the analysis of the dichotomy between conservatism and innovation below, p. 130.

3 Q. by Philip M. Burgess, *Elite Images and Foreign Policy Outcomes*, p. 104, op. cit.

4 Cf. S. Hampshire, *Thought and Action*, 1959, pp. 209–10.

5 Cf. H. and M. Sprout, *Man-Milieu Relationship Hypotheses in the Context of International Politics*, 1959.

6 Cf. A. Wolfers and L. W. Martin, *Anglo-American Tradition*, 1956, p. 20.

7 This concept that satiated basic needs lead to stability and acceptance of the *status quo* is developed in the subsequent section. It is based upon and parallel to the traditional western idea that domestic stability is best ensured by giving the largest possible portion of population a 'stake in democracy'.

8 Cf. D. Vital, *The Inequality of States*, op. cit.

9 See above, pp. 30 ff.

10 For further discussion see below pp. 148–155.

11 *Discord and Collaboration*, op. cit., pp. 73 ff.

12 For a full analysis of the problem see J. Frankel, *International Politics: Conflict and Harmony*, 1969.

9/Towards an Assessment

1 See above, pp. 142 ff.

2 Cf. R. V. Daniels, "The Chinese Revolution in Russian Perspective", *World Politics*, 1968. esp. p. 223; see also, G. Niemeyer, *An Inquiry into Soviet Neutrality*, 1956; M. Lindsay, *China and the Cold War*, 1955.

3   Cf. "The Great Withdrawal", leader, *The Times*, London, August 26, 1969.

4   A parallel can be found in an unexpressed ideological assumption of the work of British and United States courts that private interests determine public interests. When faced with a conflict, the courts take refuge in their presumed identity but examine thoroughly only the private interest and give priority to it. (Prof. W. Friedmann, q. by A. Shonfield, "The Pragmatic Illusion", *Encounter*, June 1967, p. 7.

Likewise it has been an unexpressed ideological assumption of British or United States foreign policies that the international interests of their large companies are identical with national interests; only in the post-war period has this assumption been questioned.

5   The most trenchant analysis of international organization is found in Inis L. Claude, Jr., *Swords into Plowshares*, 3rd edn. 1964.

6   Cf. *The Hindu* (newspaper), April 6, 1968.

Bibliography

Select bibliography

BEARD, CHARLES A., *The Idea of National Interest: An Analytical Study in American Foreign Policy*, Macmillan, New York 1934. The first extensive application of the concept to the analysis of United States history.

MORGENTHAU, HANS J., *Politics Among Nations: The Struggle for Power and Peace*, Knopf, New York, 1st edn. 1948, 4th edn. 1966. The classical statement of the realist school of international relations based upon the theory of power politics.

———*In Defense of the National Interest: A Critical Examination of American Foreign Policy*, Knopf, New York 1951. The application of the theories to the analysis of United States foreign policy.

OSGOOD, ROBERT E., *Ideals and Self-Interest in America's Foreign Relations: The Great Transformation of the Twentieth Century*, University of Chicago Press, Chicago 1953. The most extensive analysis by a leading representative of the idealist school.

ROSENAU, JAMES N., "National Interest", *International Encyclopaedia of the Social Sciences*, Crowell Collier and Macmillan, New York 1968. A comprehensive and acute analysis which dismisses the usefulness of the concept in political analysis.

WOLFERS, ARNOLD, *Discord and Collaboration: essays on International Politics*, Johns Hopkins Press, Baltimore 1962. An exceptionally clear example of the realist approach.

General bibliography

ARON, RAYMOND, *Peace and War*, Weidenfeld and Nicolson, London 1966.

BELOFF, M., *Foreign Policy and the Democratic Process*, Oxford University Press, London 1955.

BLACK, J. E. and THOMSON, K. W., *Foreign Policies in a World of Change*, Harper and Row, New York 1963.

BOULDING, K. E., *The Image*, University of Michigan Press, Ann Arbor 1956.

BRECHT, A., *Political Theory*, Princeton University Press, Princeton 1954.

BROOKINGS INSTITUTION, *Major Problems of United States Foreign Policy 1953–1954*, The Brookings Institution, Washington 1955.

BURGESS, P. M., *Elite Images and Foreign Policy Outcomes—a Study of Norway*, Ohio State University Press, Columbus 1968.

BURTON, J. W., *International Relations: a General Theory*, Cambridge University Press, Cambridge 1965.

———— *Systems, States, Diplomacy and Rules*, Cambridge University Press, Cambridge 1968.

CLAUDE, INIS L. Jr., *Swords into Plowshares*, University of London Press, London 1964, 3rd edn.

COOK, THOMAS I. and MOOS, M., *Power Through Purpose: The Realism of Idealism as a Basis for Foreign Policy*, Johns Hopkins Press, Baltimore 1954.

DOWNS, A., *An Economic Theory of Democracy*, Harper, New York 1957.

EASTON, D., *A Systems Analysis of Political Life*, J. Wiley, New York 1965.

FOX, ANNETTE BAKER-, *The Power of Small States: Diplomacy in World War II*, University of Chicago Press, Chicago 1959.

FRANKEL, J., *International Politics: Conflict and Harmony*, Allen Lane, The Penguin Press, London 1969.

———— *International Relations*, Oxford University Press, London and New York 1964 and rev. edn. 1969.

———— *The Making of Foreign Policy*, Oxford University Press, London and New York 1963 and 1967.

———— "National Interest: a Vindication", *The International Journal*, Toronto, Autumn 1969.

GROSS, F., *Foreign Policy Analysis*, Philosophical Library, New York 1954.

HERZ, J., *International Politics*, Columbia University Press, New York and London 1959 and 1963.

KIRK, GRAYSON L., "In Search of the National Interest", *World Politics*, 1952 5:110–15.

MACHIAVELLI, *The Discourses*, The Modern Library, New York 1950.

———— *The Prince*, The Modern Library, New York 1950.

MODELSKI, G., *A Theory of Foreign Policy*, Praeger, New York 1962.

MORGENTHAU, H. J., *Dilemmas of Politics*, University of Chicago Press, Chicago 1958.

PALMER, N. D. (ed.), *The National Interest: Alone or with Others?* American Academy of Political and Social Science, Annals, Philadelphia 1962, Vol. 282.

ROSENAU, J. N. (ed.), *International Politics and Foreign Policy*, The Free Press, New York 1967.

SCHILLING, WARNER R., "Clarification of Ends—or Which Interest is National?", *World Politics*, 1956.

SNYDER, RICHARD C., BRUCK, H. W. and SAPIN, B., *Decision-making as an Approach to the Study of International Politics*, Organizational Behaviour Section, Princeton 1954.

SPROUT, H. and M., *Foundations of National Power*, Van Nostrand, New York 1945.

———— *Man-Milieu Hypotheses in the Context of International Politics*, Princeton University Press, Princeton 1959.

VAN DYKE, V., "Values and Interests", *American Political Science Review*, 1962.

WOHLSTETTER, A., "Strength, Interests, New Technologies", *Adelphi Paper*, No. 4, Institute of Strategic Studies, London 1967.

YOUNG, R. A. (ed.), *Approaches to the Study of Politics*, Northwestern University Press, Evanston 1958. Stevens, London 1959.

Index